THE
Archive Photographs
SERIES

SURREY
COUNTY CRICKET CLUB

ERIC AND ALEC BEDSER. The Bedser twins, Eric and Alec pictured at the Oval with the famous gas holders in the background.

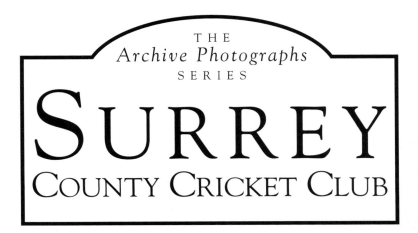

THE
Archive Photographs
SERIES

SURREY
COUNTY CRICKET CLUB

Compiled by
William A. Powell

CHALFORD

The Chalford Publishing Company
St Mary's Mill, Chalford,
Stroud, Gloucestershire, GL6 8NX

ISBN 0 7524 0390 7

Typesetting and origination by
The Chalford Publishing Company
Printed in Great Britain by
Redwood Books, Trowbridge

SURREY C.C.C. BADGE. The famous Surrey County Cricket Club badge. Although the club had been tenants of the Duchy of Cornwall since 1845 it was not until 1906 that permission was granted to use the Prince of Wales' Feathers.

Contents

JACK HOBBS AT THE WICKET.

Introduction

'On Wednesday the 29th instant will be played a famous match of cricket at Dartford Brimpth for £50 by Kent and Surrey' (Post Man 25 June 1709). This is noted to be the first cricket match in which Surrey was involved.

If the convivial meeting at The Horns tavern, Kennington, in October 1845 had been granted the power to see the outcome of their decision to provide Surrey cricket with a 'local habitation and a name' there would have been both awe and satisfaction. The sight of a packed ground at the Oval on a great occasion, a Jack Hobbs and Tom Hayward first-wicket partnership, Peter May in full attacking flight, a bowling burst from Tom Richardson, overs from Alec Bedser, Jim Laker and company and the fielding during those incredible seven county championship seasons, would have exceeded all expectations.

No county can boast a longer or richer history - mention of the game at Guildford goes back as far as 1850 - and the Oval, once a ten acre market garden, has an honoured place ever since it staged the very first home Test Match on English soil against Australia in 1880. The first county fixture was on 25 and 26 June 1846, when neighbours Kent were defeated, and the vision of Harrovian Charles Alcock, the county's first paid secretary, put the ground firmly on the sporting map. Not only did he have the initiative to arrange the first Test Match in England at the Oval, but in his joint role as Secretary of the Football Association, he dreamed up the F.A. Challenge Cup. Its first few finals, and the first home soccer internationals with Scotland and Wales, were played at Kennington Oval, and, for good measure, Alcock also arranged the first rugby internationals against Scotland and Ireland at the ground. Kerry Packer had nothing on Charles Alcock.

One hundred and fifty years on and it was imperative that the club embark on big scale developments at the Oval ready for the next century and the 1999 World Cup. After much negotiation and disappointment involving even Government Departments, Elders IXL, the Australian Brewery Group, in the name of their Foster's brand lager, offered and agreed a sponsorship deal by which the famous old ground became 'The Foster's Oval' for the fifteen year duration of the contract from October 1988. This sponsorship together with donations raised through the Ken Barrington Appeal and Save the Oval Appeal, has enabled the club to make improvements to its famous ground. These have included the Bedser, Lock and Laker Stands and the Members Pavilion. Further developments are planned to take place prior to the World Cup in 1999 thanks to the funds raised by the Surrey 150th Year Appeal, to increase the ground capacity. The only alternative to sponsorship would have been the unthinkable loss of the Oval as a Test venue, or, at worst, the ground itself. The ground remains, of course, part of the lands of the Duchy of Cornwall. In 1930 Edward, then Prince of Wales, jokingly made that plain when he saw a note pinned to the door of the Australian dressing room forbidding entry without the manager's permission, 'You can't keep me out', was his response, 'I'm your landlord!'

Surrey has often been a pacemaker of cricket. H.H. Stephenson captained the first England team to Australia, and in the late 1880s and 1890s they were seldom off the top. John Shuter was one of many outstanding captains of Surrey - general agreement is that Percy Fender was the finest of all and a length in front of Douglas Jardine - and was the first to declare an innings closed. The roll of honour of distinguished players and their deeds for Surrey could fill a volume, but the pride of place belongs to 'The Master' John Berry Hobbs, the first professional cricketer to be knighted. Jack Hobbs ennobled the art of batting, conquered all forms of newly invented bowling from swing to the googly, and left a string of records that could stand for all time. He scored 197 first-class centuries, 98 coming after the age of 40, and 61,760 runs, and as a natural number one, shared 166 first-wicket stands of 100 or more, including 66 with Andy Sandham and 40 with Tom Hayward. Twenty-eight of the stands passed 200, and in 13 days he shared opening partnerships of 428, 182, 106 and 123 before a wicket fell.

In the words of Percy Fender, Jack Hobbs was simply the best in all conditions of all time; indeed he made runs on old-style Australian gluepots and had, to an astonishing degree, that quality which separates the great from the very good, of being able to score off the good ball. Jack Hobbs hailed from Cambridge where his idol Tom Hayward lived. Tom Hayward was the first to follow Dr W.G. Grace with 100 hundreds, and was one of the elite scoring 1,000 runs in twenty seasons - before the end of May in 1890 - and totalled 3,170 in 1904 and 3,518 in 1906. A classical batsman he came from a family of cricketing perfectionists, who played for Surrey XIs. The young Jack Hobbs could have had no better mentor, and no better tribute can be imagined than to say he was even better than Tom Hayward.

Only Surrey can boast of four batsman with over 100 first-class hundreds. After Jack Hobbs, comes Andy Sandham with 107, Tom Hayward with 104 and John Edrich with 103. To find John Edrich, the efficient left hander in such company is perhaps surprising, but he had all the merits and determination of his Norfolk family and was effective for both Surrey and England. No doubt Peter May, the greatest batsman of England since 1946, and Ken Barrington, a high-ranker with 20 Test centuries and an average of almost 60 with 76 hundreds would have joined the elite club if they had played longer. Peter May's dual responsibilities as leading batsman and captain in 41 Tests for England eventually took its toll, and Ken Barrington, without an enemy in the world, suffered a second and fatal heart attack while serving as assistant manager of England at Barbados in 1981.

Way back in the 1880s the Oval took little Bobby 'The Gov'nor' Abel to its heart - no-one has overtaken his 357 not out versus Somerset in 1899 - and Tom Richardson, who used to walk to his home at Mitcham carrying his cricket bag after a day's fast bowling, was one of the game's greatest fast bowlers. Herbert Strudwick, the famed wicket-keeper, recommended to the County by a Sunday school mistress, always said Tom Richardson never wittingly bowled a short pitcher in his life. The Tom Richardson-Bill Lockwood partnership was much feared, and George Lohmann and Jack Crawford, who quarrelled with the club and went to Australia, were outstanding personalities.

For all Percy Fender's ingenuity Surrey, handicapped by the quality of home prepared pitches and sometimes by the inability to take the catches off the potent fast bowling of Alf Gover, could not manage a county championship between the wars. The first tangible success after the 1914 victory was to share the title in 1950 with Lancashire, but it was then very clear that Surrey were on the brink of high achievement. Before he started his captaincy in 1952 Stuart Surridge wrote in his diary: 'Surrey will be champions for the next five years'. How right he proved to be. Stuart Surridge was born within two miles of the Oval, and one important reason for Surrey's success was that he had grown up with many of his team; the Bedser twins Alec and

Eric, Arthur McIntyre, a superb wicket-keeper, Bernie Constable and the hitter Geoff Whittaker. His attack of Alec Bedser, an all-time great, Peter Loader, and the spinners Jim Laker and Tony Lock was virtually England's, and as a back-up all-rounder Eric Bedser was close to that class as an off-spinner. The fielding was dramatic, and Surrey played with such fire and purpose that they expected to take a wicket with every ball. Some of Stuart Surridge's declarations were so audacious that they seemed to be acts of folly, but they invariably came off, and the psychological pressure alone was often too much for the opposition.

Surrey raced to championships with bowlers who stood out at Test level, let alone at county. Jim Laker was arguably the best off-spinner of all time with 19 wickets for England versus Australia at Old Trafford, Manchester in 1961, a record never likely to be beaten. When Stuart Surridge retired in triumph, Peter May extended the run to seven county championships and in 1971 Micky Stewart, later England's team manager, completed Surrey's eighteenth outright county championship success.

Little has been achieved in the championship since, although Surrey finished runners-up in 1973 to Hampshire and in 1980 to Middlesex. However with the introduction of One Day cricket the county have had more success. Under the captaincy of John Edrich, Surrey beat Leicestershire at Lord's to win the Benson & Hedges Cup in 1974 and under the leadership of Roger Knight now secretary of M.C.C. they beat Warwickshire at Lord's to win the NatWest Trophy in 1982.

This introduction cannot be concluded without me thanking the many who have assisted me with this work, all those who have made some contribution are included in the acknowledgements.

William A. Powell
Hemel Hempstead
Hertfordshire
April 1996

DOUGLAS JARDINE AND PERCY FENDER. Douglas Jardine and Percy Fender who both captained Surrey during the period 1921 to 1933 with little success.

THE OVAL 1960. This aerial view of the Oval was taken during a county match.

Acknowledgements

The author would like to thank the following who have assisted in a variety of ways in the preparation of this book including the use of illustrations other than those from the author's own collection:

Alex Bannister, David Buxton, the late Ron Harries, Vic Lewis, the late Bob Jones, David Hart, Mike Tarr, Peter Powell, John Lodge, Steven Johns, Glyn Woodman and Jeff Hancock.

I acknowledge the sources of the illustrations which are many and include the Surrey County Cricket Club, F.C. Dick, County Print Services, Pamlin Prints, Frith's, Walker's Studio, the Harries family collection, the Vic Lewis collection and my own collection of picture postcards. Apologies are offered to anyone whose photographs have inadvertently been used without due acknowledgement.

Bibliography

Who's Who of Cricketers, Hamlyn 1993 Philip Bailey, Philip Thorn, Peter Wynne-Thomas. *The History of Surrey County Cricket Club*, Christopher Helm 1989, David Lemmon. *The Story of the Oval*, Cornish 1949, Louis Palgrave. *Surrey County Cricket Club 1845-1945* Centenary Souvenir, Home Publishing Co. 1945. *My Life Story*, The Star Publications 1935, Jack Hobbs. *Cricket of Today and Yesterday* Volumes I and II, Blackwood, Percy Cross Standing. *The Cricket Annual 1892*, Frank Fawcett 1892, William Dewar. *Forty Seasons of First-Class Cricket*, John Heywood Limited 1909, R.G. Barlow. *Surrey Cricket : Its History and Associations*, Longmans & Co. 1902, Lord Alverstone and C.W. Alcock. *Famous Cricketers and Cricket Grounds*, Hudson & Kearns 1895, C.W. Alcock. *Defending The Ashes*, Chapman and Hall Ltd. 1921, P.G.H. Fender. *Surrey Cricketers 1839-1980* A.C.S. 1980, Peter Wynne-Thomas. *The Surrey Story*, Stanley Paul 1957, Gordon Ross. *A History of County Cricket - Surrey*, Arthur Barker 1971, Gordon Ross. *The Wisden Guide To Cricket Grounds*, Stanley Paul 1992, William Powell. *England Test Cricketers*, Collins Willow 1989, Bill Frindall. *Cricket Grounds Then and Now*, Dial House 1994, William Powell. *James Lillywhites Annuals* 1882 to 1900, C.W. Alcock. *The Cricketer International Magazine* 1921 to 1995. *Cricket Weekly Record* 1882 to 1913. *World of Cricket* 1914. Surrey County Cricket Club Yearbooks 1948 to 1995.

One
The Early Years

THE OLD SURREY TEAM 1852. Standing, left to right: W. Mortlock, T. Lockyer, H.H. Stephenson, W. Caffyn, G. Griffith, Mr E. Dowson, Mr F.P. Miller, Mr C.G. Lane, Mr F. Burbidge, Julius Caesar and T. Sewell. They played 7 matches in 1852 winning 2 drawing 1 and losing 4 under the leadership of Mr F.P. Miller.

SURREY TEAM 1883. Back row, left to right: R. Abel, Mr C.E. Horner, Mr M.P. Bowden, Mr E.J. Diver, Mr W.W. Read. Front row, left to right: E. Barratt, Mr K.J. Key, R. Henderson, Mr J. Shuter (captain), J.M. Read, Mr W.E. Roller. Under the leadership of Mr J. Shuter, Surrey played 21 matches during the season winning 10, drawing 5 and losing 6.

SURREY TEAM 1887. Back row, left to right: G.G. Jones, J.M. Read, Mr W.W. Read, Mr W.E. Roller, J. Beaumont (standing), Mr M.P. Bowden, G.A. Lohmann and H. Wood. Front row, left to right: R. Henderson, R. Abel and T. Bowley. Led by J. Shuter in 1887 Surrey played 19 matches, winning 14, drawing 2 and losing 3.

'FELIX' MR NICHOLAS WANOSTROCHT. Born at Camberwell, London in 1804 Nicholas 'Felix' Wanostrocht, the brother in law of H.T. Reed (M.C.C.), was a left-arm under-arm bowler and late order left-handed batsman. He represented his native Surrey 23 times between 1846 and 1852, scoring 659 runs (av. 17.81) with a highest score of 82. He also played 55 matches for neighbours Kent between 1834 and 1852. He also invented the `Catapulta' bowling machine and tubular India rubber batting gloves. He died at Wimborne, Dorset in 1876.

SURREY TEAM 1888. Back row, left to right: Mr M.P. Bowden, Mr K.J. Key, J. Beaumont, H. Wood. Middle row, left to right: Mr W.W. Read, J.M. Read, Mr J. Shuter (captain), G.A. Lohmann and T. Bowley. Front row, left to right: R. Abel and R. Henderson. Under the leadership of Mr J. Shuter, Surrey played 19 matches during the season winning 13, drawing 3 and losing 3.

WILLIAM CAFFYN. Born at Reigate in 1828, William Caffyn, the nephew of Walter (Surrey), was a right-handed middle order batsman and right-arm medium bowler. Representing Surrey in 89 matches from 1849 to 1873 he took 321 wickets (av. 13.39) with a best of 8 for 25, he also scored 3,226 runs (av. 23.20) with 2 centuries including a top score of 103 not out and he held 72 catches. He also represented Kent, Lancashire and New South Wales and he toured abroad twice with Stephenson and Parr to Australia in 1861/62 and 1863/64 and to America in 1859. He died at Reigate in 1919.

SURREY TEAM 1892. Back row, left to right: Vetch (umpire), T. Richardson, G.A. Lohmann, E.C. Streatfield, F. Boyington (scorer), K.J. Key, (umpire). Middle row, left to right: H. Wood, R. Henderson, J. Shuter (captain), W.H. Lockwood, W.W. Read. Front row, left to right: R. Abel and J.M. Read. Captained by J. Shuter, the county achieved the championship for the third successive season with 13 wins, a single draw and just 2 defeats.

SURREY TEAM 1894. Back row, left to right: J.M. Read, T. Richardson, G.W. Ayres, F.E. Smith. Middle row, left to right: H. Wood, W.H. Lockwood, K.J. Key (captain), W. Brockwell and W.W. Read. Front row, left to right: T.W. Hayward, R. Abel and A.E. Street, K.J. Key. The team that led the county to the championship in 1894 with 13 victories.

THE RIGHT HON SIR SPENCER C.B. PONSONBY-FANE GCB. Born in Mayfair, London in 1824, Sir Spencer Ponsonby-Fane, was a right-handed top order batsman and good deep fieldsman. He represented Surrey in just 3 first-class matches from 1844 to 1853, scoring only 12 runs and taking a single catch. He later played a single match for Middlesex in 1862 and he played his remaining 58 first-class matches for M.C.C. and Ireland. He was a prominent committee member of M.C.C., Surrey and Somerset. With one of his brothers and J.L. Baldwin he established the I Zingari club in 1845. Apart from his work as a cricket administrator he held many important posts including Private Secretary in the Government of the time. He died at Brympton D'Evercy near Yeovil, Somerset in 1915.

SURREY CRICKETERS AUTOGRAPHS 1890-1910. This interesting collection of Surrey players autographs was collected during the period 1890 to 1910 and includes; D.L.A. Jephson, K.J. Key, H.D.G. Leveson-Gower, W. Davis, A. Marshal, Edward Pooley, Fred Stedman, Lord Dalmeny, N.A. Knox, J.H. Gordon, Fred Holland, H. Strudwick, T. Rushby, W.S. Lees, J.B. Hobbs, W.C. Smith, J.N. Crawford, Ernest G. Hayes, Robert Abel, W. Brockwell, T. Richardson, W.H. Lockwood, H. Wood, T. Hayward, C. Baldwin and James Street.

SURREY TEAM 1895. Back row, left to right: W.H. Lockwood, T.W. Hayward, J.M. Read and W. Brockwell. Middle row, left to right: W.W. Read, T. Richardson, K.J. Key (captain), R. Abel and G.A. Lohmann. Front row, left to right H.D.G. Leveson-Gower and H. Wood (wkt-kpr.). County champions for the fifth time with 17 wins during the season.

CHARLES W. ALCOCK. Born in 1842, Charles Alcock was secretary of the Surrey County Cricket Club from 1872 to 1907. During this time he arranged the Test matches between England and Australia including the Ashes Tests of 1882. The father of the modern sport he was also the secretary and treasurer of the Football Association from 1870 to 1896 and vice-president from 1896 to 1907. He organised the first international association football matches between England and Scotland in 1872 at the Oval and he initiated the Football Association Challenge Cup competition in 1871. He captained the first winning side of the F.A. Cup, the Wanderers to a 1-0 victory over the Royal Engineers at the Oval in 1872. The Oval in fact staged every F.A. Cup Final between 1874 and 1892. Present league clubs to have won the trophy at the Oval include Blackburn Rovers, Aston Villa, West Bromwich Albion and Preston North End. An author of both cricket and football publications, he died in 1907.

SURREY TEAM 1898. Back row, left to right: W.S. Lees, T. Richardson, E.G. Hayes, and H. Wood. Middle row, left to right W.H. Lockwood, Mr H.B. Richardson, Mr K.J. Key (captain), Mr F.P. Knox and W. Brockwell. Front row, left to right: R. Abel, Mr N. Miller. Surrey finished fourth in the county championship with 11 wins, 9 draws and 4 defeats under the captaincy of K.J. Key.

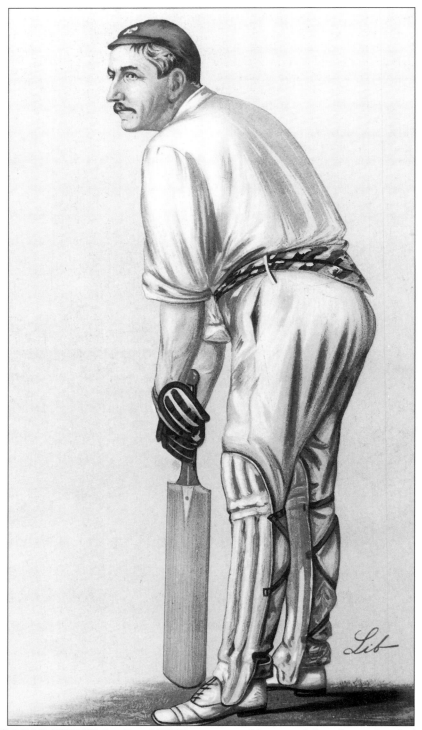

WALTER READ WW. Walter Read 'WW' was painted by artist Lib and issued with the *Vanity Fair* magazine in 1888.

DIGBY JEPHSON. Born at Brixton, London in 1871, Digby Jephson was an opening right-handed batsman, right-arm fast-medium bowler who changed to under-arm lobs in 1892. He represented Cambridge University between 1890 and 1892 where he obtained Blues in each year before commencing his career with Surrey. He represented the county in 165 first-class matches from 1894 to 1904, scoring 6,566 runs (av. 32.02) with 9 centuries including a top score of 213 versus Derbyshire at the Oval in 1900. He also took 249 wickets (av. 23.08) which a best of 7 for 51 and he held 82 catches. He achieved 1,000 runs in a season four times and his best season was 1900 when he scored 1,952 runs (av. 41.53). He took over the captaincy of the county from K.J. Key in 1900 before handing over to L. Walker in 1903. He died at Cambridge in 1926.

SIR KINGSMILL JAMES KEY. Born at Streatham in 1864, the cousin of L.H. Gay (Hampshire and Somerset), Kingsmill James Key was an attacking middle order right-handed batsman and off-break bowler. Having learnt his cricket at Clifton College, he went onto Oxford University where he obtained Blues in all four years between 1884-87 for cricket and in one year a Blue at rugby football. During his last year he scored his only double century 281 versus Middlesex at Chiswick Park. Representing Surrey from 1882 to 1904 in 288 first-class matches, he scored 9,654 runs (av. 26.23) with 8 centuries and a top score of 179. He led the county between 1894-99 to three championships and he toured abroad to North America twice in 1886 and 1891 and India in 1902/03 with the Oxford University Authentics. His last first-class appearance was for Leveson-Gower's XI in 1909. He received a knighthood and died at Wittersham, Kent in 1932 from blood poisoning after an insect bite.

19

ALFRED LUCAS. Born at Westminster, London in 1857, Alfred Lucas, the cousin of C.F. (Hampshire), was a right-handed opening batsman, slow round-arm bowler and good fieldsman. Schooled at Uppingham, he achieved Blues all four years whilst at Cambridge University from 1875 to 1878. He played 41 first-class matches for the county from 1874 to 1882, scoring 1,721 runs (av. 24.58), he took 62 wickets (av. 16.30) and he held 31 catches. He later represented Middlesex in 11 matches from 1883 to 1888 and Essex in 98 matches from 1894 to 1907 before retiring from the game. He played 5 Tests for England between 1878/79 to 1884, touring once to Australia in 1878/79. He captained Essex from 1892 to 1894 and jointly in 1901. He died at Great Waltham, Essex in 1923.

SURREY TEAM 1899. Back row, left to right: T. Mycroft (umpire), W.S. Lees, W.H. Lockwood, T. Richardson, W. Brockwell, E.G. Hayes, H. Wood and W. Hearn (umpire). Middle row, left to right: H.C. Pretty, D.L.A. Jephson, K.J. Key (captain), T.W. Hayward, R. Abel. Front row, left to right: F. Stedman and E.H.L. Nice. County champions for the sixth time with 10 wins, 14 draws and just 2 defeats.

WILLIAM BROCKWELL. Born at Kingston-upon-Thames in 1865, nephew of George (Surrey), William Brockwell was a stylish right-handed opening batsman, right-arm fast bowler and good slip fieldsman. He played 314 first-class matches for the county between 1886 and 1903 scoring 13,285 runs (av. 27.00) with a top score of 225 versus Hampshire at the Oval in 1897. He also bagged 553 wickets (av. 24.73) with a best of 8 for 22 and he held 250 catches. He represented England in 7 Tests from 1893 to 1899 and he toured abroad twice with Read and Stoddart's teams. He completed the double in 1899 which was his best season and after retiring from the game he fell on hard times and subsequently died in abject poverty at Richmond, Surrey in 1935.

VIVIAN CRAWFORD. Born in Leicester in 1871, Vivian Crawford was a hard-hitting middle order right-handed batsman and right-arm fast bowler. He was educated at the Whitgift School where he scored 1,340 runs during the 1897 season. He represented Surrey in 110 first-class matches between 1896 and 1902 before moving north to his native Leicestershire where he was appointed secretary and for whom he also played 165 matches between 1903 and 1910. For Surrey he accumulated 4,280 runs (av. 28.72) with 8 centuries including a highest score of 159 and he held 64 catches. He achieved 1,000 runs in a season five times and his best year was 1901 when he scored 1,511 runs (av. 32.14). Son of J.C. (Kent), brother of J.N. (Surrey and South Australia) and R.T. (Leicestershire) and nephew of F.F. (Kent), he emigrated to Ceylon to become a tea-planter, returning to serve in the First World War. He later died of pneumonia at Merton, Surrey in 1922.

BILL LOCKWOOD. Born at Old Radford, Nottingham in 1868, Bill Lockwood represented his native Nottinghamshire between 1886 and 1887 before his move to South London to partner Tom Richardson in attack at the Oval. A high class right-handed all-rounder he assisted Surrey to six championships in ten seasons. Playing 305 first-class matches for the county between 1889 and 1904 he took 1,182 wickets (av. 17.99) with a best of 9 for 59 and he scored 9,299 runs (av. 22.51) including 14 centuries with a highest score of 165. He appeared in 12 Tests for England, touring abroad once to Australia in 1894/95. He took 43 wickets (av. 20.55) with a best of 7 for 71 versus Australia at the Oval in 1899 and he scored 231 runs with a top score of 52 not out. He died at his Nottingham home in 1932.

GEORGE LOHMANN. Born at Kensington, London in 1865 George Lohmann was a hostile right-handed all-rounder. A tall robust figure he was one of the most economical and penetrative bowlers to have played cricket and he was a key performer in the county's five championships in six years after the competition had been constituted in 1890. Playing 186 first-class matches for the county between 1884 and 1896 he scored 5,070 runs (av. 20.77) with 2 centuries, took 1,221 wickets (av. 13.19) with a best of 9 for 67 and he held 203 catches. He achieved 200 wickets in a season in three consecutive seasons. Representing England in 18 Tests he bagged 112 wickets (av. 10.75) with a best of 9 for 28 versus South Africa at Johannesburg in 1895/96. Touring abroad four times he emigrated to South Africa in 1896 after playing two seasons for Western Province in Cape Town. He returned to England in 1901 as manager of the South African team but he died aged 37 on his return home at Worcester, Cape Province.

JOHN SHUTER. Born at Thornton Heath, Surrey in 1855, John Shuter, the brother of L.A. (Surrey) and uncle of L.R.W.A. (M.C.C.), John Shuter was a stylish right-handed opening batsman and exceptional fieldsman. He schooled at Winchester and after playing a single match with Kent in 1874 moved to the Oval where, he represented the county in 274 first-class matches between 1877 and 1909. He scored 9,369 runs (av. 21.89) with 8 centuries, including a top score of 135 and he also held 141 catches. Captaining the county from 1880 to 1893, he was secretary of the county in 1920 until his death at Blackheath, London that year. He played a single Test for England in 1888. His best season was 1884 when he scored 968 runs (av. 26.88). He died at Blackheath, London in 1920.

H.D.G. LEVESON-GOWER. Born at Titsey Place, Surrey in 1873, Henry 'Shrimp' Leveson-Gower was a right-handed middle order batsman, leg-break bowler and good cover fieldsman. Learning his early cricket whilst at Winchester, he progressed to Oxford University where he obtained Blues for all four years between 1893 and 1896. He later represented Surrey in 122 first-class matches between 1895 and 1920, scoring 3,308 runs (av. 22.50) with a top score of 155 and also held 38 catches. Captaining Oxford in 1896 and Surrey between 1908 and 1910 he led the M.C.C. team to South Africa in 1909/10. Playing 3 Tests on that tour he scored 95 runs (av. 23.75) with a top score of 31. He later ran his own first-class XI, and after retiring became a noted cricket administrator, including periods as a Test selector and committee member and president of Surrey between 1929 to 1939. In 1953 he was knighted for his services to cricket. He died at Kensington, London in 1954.

Two
The Golden Age

DIGBY JEPHSON THE LOBSTER. Digby Jephson 'The Lobster' was painted by artist Spy and issued with the *Vanity Fair* magazine in 1902.

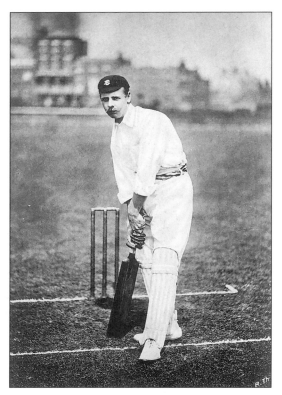

TOM HAYWARD. The tall well-built right-handed Tom Hayward, was born at Cambridge in 1871. Playing 593 first-class matches for the county between 1893 and 1914 he amassed 36,175 runs (av. 42.40) with 88 centuries and a top score of 315 not out versus Lancashire at the Oval in 1898. He also took 436 wickets (av. 21.42) with a best of 8 for 89 and he held 420 catches. During his illustrious career he opened the batting for Surrey with fellow Cambridgeshire man Jack Hobbs. Achieving the double in 1897, his best season was 1906 when he scored 3,518 runs, a record which survived until beaten by Denis Compton in 1947. Representing England in 35 Tests he scored 1,999 runs (av. 34.46) with a highest score of 137 versus Australia at the Oval in 1899 and he took 14 wickets (av. 36.71). He was the first professional and only the second batsman after Dr W.G. Grace to record one hundred first-class hundreds. He died at Cambridge in 1939.

LORD DALMENY. Lord Dalmeny 'In his father's steps' was painted by artist Spy and issued with the *Vanity Fair* magazine in 1904.

SURREY TEAM 1901. Back row, left to right: W.S. Lees, T. Richardson, R. Abel, T.W. Hayward, E.G. Hayes, F.C. Holland and F. Boyington (scorer). Middle row, left to right: E.M. Dowson, H.D.G. Leveson-Gower, D.L.A. Jephson (captain), L. Walker and V.F.S. Crawford. Front row, left to right: F. Stedman. Surrey ended the season in a disappointing eleventh place in the championship with 7 wins, 14 draws and 6 defeats.

BOBBY ABEL. Bobby Abel 'Bobby' was painted by artist Spy and issued with the *Vanity Fair* magazine in 1902.

SURREY TEAM 1902. Back row, left to right: W.S. Lees, T. Richardson, T.W. Hayward, F.C. Holland, E.G. Hayes and F. Boyington (scorer). Middle row, left to right: E.M. Dowson, H.D.G. Leveson-Gower, D.L.A. Jephson (captain), V.F.S. Crawford and L. Walker. Front row, left to right: F. Stedman, R. Abel. Under the captaincy of D.L.A. Jephson Surrey finished fourth in the championship with 8 victories, 15 draws and 5 defeats.

VANITY FAIR *Surrey*

TOM HAYWARD. Tom Hayward 'Tom' was painted by artist Spy and issued with the *Vanity Fair* magazine in 1906.

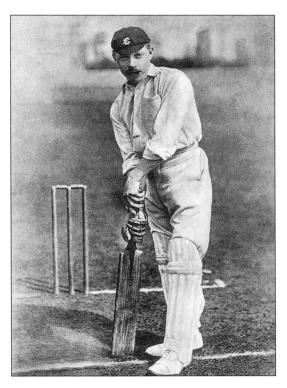

BOBBY ABEL. Born at Rotherhithe in 1857 and nicknamed 'The Guv'nor' the diminutive Bobby Abel was a right-handed batsman, right-arm slow bowler and outstanding slip fieldsman. In 1899 he hit a then ground record of 357 not out for Surrey versus Somerset at the Oval out of a county record total of 811 all out. Representing the county in 514 matches from 1881 to 1904 he scored 27,605 runs (av. 36.61) with 64 centuries, took 256 wickets (av. 23.30) with a best of 6 for 15 and he held 492 catches. By far his best season was 1901 when he hit 3,309 runs although he did pass 2,000 runs in a season 8 times. Playing for England in 13 Tests between 1888 and 1902 he toured abroad twice and amassed 744 runs (av. 37.20) with a top score of 132 not out versus Australia at Sydney in 1891/92. He died at Stockwell in 1936.

LORD DALMENY. Born in Mayfair, Westminster, London in 1882, Lord Dalmeny (succeeded as 6th Earl of Rosebery in 1929), was a middle order right-handed batsman and right-arm fast bowler. He attended Eton and played for Buckinghamshire from 1899 to 1901 and 2 matches for Middlesex in 1902 before moving to Surrey in 1903 for whom he played 94 first-class matches. During this time he also captained the county between 1905 and 1907, scored 3,386 runs (av. 23.19) with 2 centuries including a top score of 138 and he held 42 catches. His best season was 1907 when he amassed 1,150 runs (av. 25.55). He also played for Scotland in 1905 and was the father of Lord Dalmeny (Middlesex) and brother-in-law of C.N. Bruce (Middlesex). When he died at Mentmore House, near Tring Hertfordshire in 1974 he left £9,650,986 net.

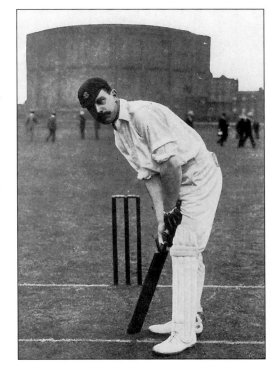

The Surrey Captains.

THE SURREY CAPTAINS. This cartoon by 'Gil' illustrates 'The Surrey Captains' during the early part of the 1904 season when Surrey had no fixed captain until John E. Raphael was appointed in August 1904 for the remainder of the season.

SURREY TEAM 1904. Back row, left to right: A. Boyington (scorer), L.M.H. Gooder, E.H.L. Nice, W.C. Smith, A. Baker and F. Stedman. Middle row, left to right: T.W. Hayward, H.C. McDonell, Lord Dalmeny (acting captain), J.E. Raphael, F.C. Holland. Front row, left to right: J.H. Moulder and W.E. Davis. They won just 6 matches during the season finishing in a disappointing eleventh place in the championship.

SURREY TEAM 1905. Back row, left to right: H. Strudwick, A. Baker, M.T. Jackson, F.C. Holland, E.H.L. Nice, J.B. Hobbs and W.E. Davis. Front row, left to right: E.G. Hayes, N.A. Knox, Lord Dalmeny (captain), T.W. Hayward and W.S. Lees. Final Championship position was fourth with 14 victories.

WALTER LEES. Born at Sowerby Bridge, Yorkshire in 1924, Walter Lees was a hard-hitting lower order batsman and right-arm medium-fast bowler. He represented the county in 343 first-class matches from 1896 to 1911, scoring 7,237 runs (av. 17.23) with 2 centuries including a top score of 137, took 1,331 wickets (av. 21.44) with a best of 9 for 81 versus Sussex at the Saffrons, Eastbourne in 1905 and he held 118 catches. He achieved 100 wickets in a season seven times with his best season being 1905 when he bagged 193 wickets (av. 18.01). He represented England in 5 Tests on the M.C.C. tour to South Africa in 1905/06 when his best haul was 6 for 78 at Johannesburg during the third Test Match. He died at West Hartlepool, County Durham of pneumonia in 1924.

SURREY TEAM 1906. Back row, left to right; H. Strudwick, A. Baker, A. Marshal, F.C. Holland, E.H.L. Nice, J.B. Hobbs and J.N. Crawford. Front row, left to right: E.G. Hayes, N.A. Knox, Lord Dalmeny (captain), T.W. Hayward and W.S. Lees. Lord Dalmeny, in his second season as captain, led the county to third in the championship with 18 victories.

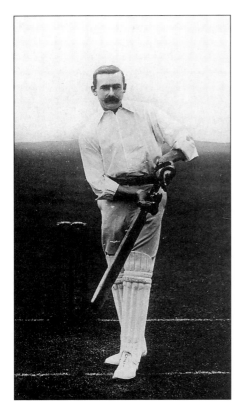

ERNEST HAYES. Born at Peckham, London in 1876, Ernest Hayes was a middle order right-handed batsman, leg-break bowler and good slip fieldsman. He represented Surrey in 500 first-class matches between 1896 and 1919, scoring 25,062 runs (av. 33.10) with 45 hundreds including a top score of 276 versus Hampshire at the Oval in 1909, took 473 wickets (av. 26.97) with a best of 8 for 22 and he held 561 catches. He achieved 1,000 runs in a season six times and his best season was 1906 when he amassed 2,309 runs (av. 45.27). Playing 5 Tests for England between 1905/06 and 1912 he achieved very little and during the tour of Australia in 1907/08 he was not selected for any Tests. He also represented London County at Crystal Palace in 1903 and after retiring became chief coach for Leicestershire between 1923 and 1928 and then at the Oval from 1929 to 1934. He died at West Dulwich, London in 1953.

BILL HITCH. Born at Radcliffe, Lancashire in 1886, Bill Hitch was a hard-hitting lower order batsman, right-arm fast bowler and useful short-leg fieldsman. He represented Surrey in 305 first-class matches from 1907 to 1925 during which time he scored 6,765 runs (av. 17.70) with 3 centuries including a highest innings of 107, took 1,232 wickets (av. 21.55) with a best of 8 for 38 and he held 204 catches. He achieved 100 wickets in a season seven times with a best of 174 wickets (av. 18.55) in 1913 and with the bat he hit 1,061 (av. 31.20) in 1921. An important bowler for Surrey, he achieved little in his 7 Tests for England between 1911/12 and 1921 and his two tours to Australia in 1911/12 and 1920/21. He officiated as a first-class umpire from 1932 to 1936 including three Tests in India in 1933/34 and he died at Runmey, Cardiff in 1965.

MY CHOICE? THE "FORCE" WATERPROOF BALL

J.W. Hitch

SURREY

SURREY VERSUS WARWICKSHIRE AT THE OVAL. Tom Hayward batting during the County's second innings whilst reaching his 100 against Warwickshire at the Oval on Tuesday 11 May 1909. Also in the photograph are bowler Syd Santall, non striking batsman Jack Hobbs, wicket-keeper Arthur Lilley and umpire J. Moss. Tom Hayward and Jack Hobbs opened Surrey's second innings scoring 352 for the first wicket in three and three-quarter hours. Tom Hayward scored 204 not out and Jack Hobbs 159 by the time the innings was declared closed at 400 for 4. Surrey (242 and 400 for 4 dec.) beat Warwickshire (155 and 316) by 171 runs in this remarkable match.

33

LORD DALMENY AT THE OVAL 1912. Left to right: G.L. Jessop (Gloucestershire), G.W. Beldham (Middlesex), A.E. Lawton (Somerset) and Lord Dalmeny watching a match at the Oval during the Triangular Series of 1912.

SURREY TEAM 1909. Inset, top, left to right: Lord Dalmeny and N.A. Knox. Back row, left to right: H. Strudwick (wkt-kpr.), W.C. Smith, A. Marshal, T. Rushby, J.B. Hobbs and W.S. Lees. Front row, left to right: W.E. Davis, T.W. Hayward, J.W. Crawford, H.D.G. Leveson-Gower (captain), E.G. Hayes and F.C. Holland. Henry Leveson-Gower guided the county to fifth in the championship with 16 wins, 7 draws and 7 defeats.

THE SURREY TEAM.

SURREY TEAM 1911. Standing, left to right: E.G. Hayes, T.W. Hayward, T. Rushby, A. Ducat, M.C. Bird (captain), W.A. Spring, W.C. Smith, J.B. Hobbs, H. Strudwick, J.W. Hitch and W.J. Abel. The county finished the season eleventh in the championship with 15 wins.

SUSSEX VERSUS SURREY AT HOVE. The first ball of the match was bowled by W.C. Smith of Surrey to R. Relf of Sussex at the County Cricket Ground, Hove on Thursday 24th August, 1911. The result of the match was a victory to Surrey by 8 wickets thanks to 151 by M.C. Bird, the Surrey captain, and match figures of 9 for 120 by J.W. Hitch.

WIMBLEDON & DISTRICT TEAM. The Wimbledon & District XI for the Annual Hospital Charity Cricket Match which was played at Wimbledon on 28 September 1912.

MR J.B. HOBBS TEAM. Mr J.B. Hobbs' XI for the Wimbledon Annual Hospital Charity Cricket match which was played at Wimbledon on 28 September 1912. This picture includes some fourteen county players from the counties of Surrey, Sussex, Middlesex, Kent and Worcestershire.

WILLIAM ABEL. Born at South Bermondsey in 1887, the son of Robert (Surrey) and brother of Thomas Ernest (Surrey and Glamorgan), William Abel was a hard hitting right-handed batsman, right-arm fast medium, later leg-break and googly bowler and good slip fieldsman. Representing the county between 1909 and 1926 he played 170 first-class matches scoring 4,984 runs (av. 23.07) with a top score of 117. He also took 184 wickets (av. 30.89) with a best of 5 for 28 and he held 146 catches. Serving in the First World War when his health deteriorated he died aged 46 at Stockwell, London in 1934.

NEVILLE KNOX. Born at Clapham, London in 1884, Neville Knox, the brother of F.P. (Surrey) and brother-in-law of C. Palmer (Middlesex), he was a lower order right-handed batsman and right-arm fast bowler. Schooled at Dulwich College, he represented Surrey in 73 first-class matches from 1904 to 1910. He scored 670 runs (av. 8.81) and bagged 347 wickets (av. 20.94) with a best of 8 for 48. He played 2 Tests for England in 1907 versus South Africa with a best of 2 for 39. He took 100 wickets in a season, twice with a best of 144 wickets (av. 19.63) in 1906. His last first-class match was for the Army in 1919. He died at Surbiton in 1935.

SURREY VERSUS YORKSHIRE AT THE OVAL. George Hirst of Yorkshire bowling to Tom Hayward of Surrey during the county championship match at the Oval on Friday 20 August 1909. Also in the photograph are wicket-keeper David Hunter, backward square-leg David

Denton, non striking batsman Jack Hobbs and umpire G. Webb. Surrey (273 and 62) beat Yorkshire (223 and 26) in this game by 86 runs. The dismissal of Yorkshire for 26 was at that time the White Rose county's lowest ever score until this record was broken in 1965.

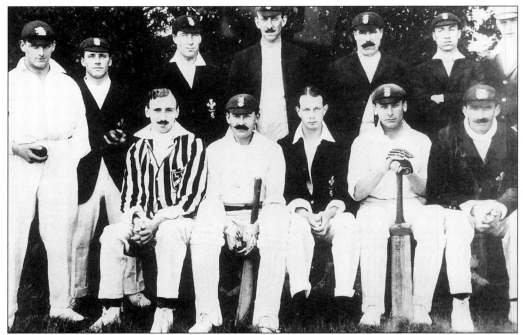

SURREY TEAM 1914. Standing, left to right: J.W. Hitch, H. Strudwick, A. Ducat, T. Rushby, E.G. Goatly, A. Sandham and W.J. Abel. Sitting, left to right: P.G.H. Fender, E.G. Hayes, C.T.A. Wilkinson (captain), J.B. Hobbs, W.A. Smith. Under the leadership of C.T.A. Wilkinson, Surrey won the county championship for the seventh time, winning 15, drawing 9 and losing just 2.

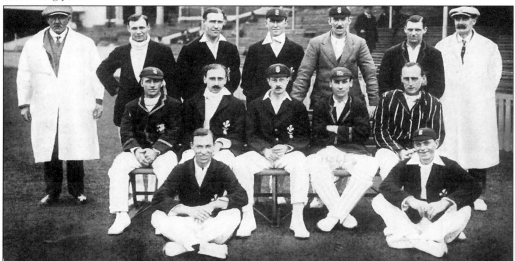

SURREY TEAM 1919. Back row, left to right: umpire (unknown), J.W. Hitch, A. Ducat, W.C. Smith, T. Rushby, D.J. Knight, umpire (unknown). Middle row, left to right: H. Strudwick, P.G.H. Fender, C.T.A. Wilkinson (captain), J.B. Hobbs and E.C. Kirk. Front row, left to right: A. Sandham and W.J. Abel. Under the leadership of C.T.A. Wilkinson, Surrey played 20 championship matches during the season winning 7, drawing 10 and losing 3. The county finished fourth in the championship at the end of the first season after the First World War.

Three
The Master

HOBBS AND THE GOOGLY. Jack Hobbs the Master seen here smothering the Googly.

YOUNG JACK HOBBS. The young 'Master' photographed in Cambridge before representing Surrey C.C.C.

JACK HOBBS WALKING OUT TO BAT. Jack Hobbs playing for Surrey against arch rivals Middlesex at Lord's Cricket Ground on Saturday, Monday and Tuesday 28th, 30th and 31st August 1926. During this match he recorded his highest score of 316 not out, which remained a ground record at Lord's until 1991 when Graham Gooch scored 333 for England versus India in a Test Match.

JACK HOBBS PLAYING THE CUT. A right-handed opening batsman, Jack Hobbs scored more runs than any other cricketer in the history of the game. During his career which spanned from 1905 to 1934 he scored a total of 61,237 first-class runs (av. 50.65).

JACK HOBBS AT THE OVAL. Jack Hobbs' best season for the county was 1914 when he amassed 2,499 runs (av. 54.52), despite also achieving 2,000 or more runs in a season in 1913, 1919, 1925 and 1928. During the 1914 season he scored 183 out of a team total of just 224 versus Warwickshire at the Oval and scored centuries in three successive innings versus Kent (Blackheath), Nottinghamshire (The Oval) and Worcestershire (Worcester).

THE "FORCE" BAT IS THE BEST.

JB. Hobbs.

SURREY.

JACK HOBBS ADVERTISES 'FORCE' BATS. Jack Hobbs regularly used Force Cricket Bats and he is seen here on an advertising postcard stating that the 'Force' bat is the best.

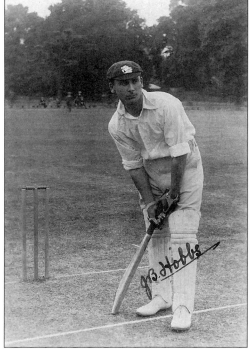

JACK HOBBS AT THE WICKET. Making his Test debut for England at Melbourne in 1907/08. Jack Hobbs scored fifteen Test hundreds and twenty-eight Test fifties. Twelve of his fifteen hundreds were scored against Australia. His highest Test score abroad was 187 versus South Africa at Cape Town in 1909/10 and versus Australia at Adelaide in 1911/12.

JACK HOBBS. During his career at the Oval, Jack Hobbs scored hundreds in each innings of a match six times, scored four centuries in successive innings in 1920 and 1925, scored centuries before lunch seventeen times and hit 1,000 runs in a season twenty-four times. Holding the highest first-wicket partnership with Andy Sandham of 428, he also held the record for the highest second wicket partnership with E.G. Hayes of 371 versus Hampshire at the Oval in 1909 when the county scored 645 for 4 in 320 minutes, the championship record for a single day.

JACK HOBBS
SURREY & ENGLAND XI.

JACK HOBBS SURREY AND ENGLAND. Playing a total of 826 first-class matches during his career Jack Hobbs amassed 197 first-class centuries, more than any other cricketer has achieved.

JACK HOBBS CERAMIC PLAQUE.
Illustrated here is a ceramic plaque of
Jack Hobbs walking out to bat at Lord's.
It was produced by New Hall Pottery in
1930.

JACK HOBBS TAKING GUARD. The
eldest of 12 children, born at Barnwell,
Cambridge in 1882 Jack Hobbs was without
doubt the most accomplished batsman of his
time. He served in the R.A.F. during the First
World War and after retiring from the game
in 1934. He was knighted for his services to
cricket in Queen Elizabeth's Coronation Year
1953 and became the first professional
cricketer to have this honour bestowed upon
him. He died at Hove, Sussex in 1963.

JACK HOBBS TAKING TO THE FIELD WHILST ON TOUR WITH ENGLAND.

JACK HOBBS WEARING HIS
SURREY BLAZER AND CAP. Making
his Surrey debut at 22 years versus Essex
at the Oval on Thursday, Friday and
Saturday 4th, 5th and 6th May 1905.
The slim, agile, medium height Jack
Hobbs scored 137 before lunch and was
duly awarded his county cap during the
luncheon interval by his captain Lord
Dalmeny.

JACK HOBBS OF SURREY. Playing 598 first-class matches for Surrey, Jack Hobbs accumulated 43,554 runs (av. 49.71) for the county with 144 centuries. He also took 86 wickets (av. 22.65) with a best of 7 for 56 and he held 239 catches.

JACK HOBBS AT THE OVAL IN 1930.

JACK HOBBS'S HIGHEST FIRST WICKET PARTNERSHIP. In front of the Oval scoreboard after the record first wicket partnership of 428 shared between Jack Hobbs 232 and Andy Sandham 183 versus Oxford University at the Oval on 23 and 24 June 1926.

JACK HOBBS PHOTOGRAPHED AT HARRODS IN LONDON.

JACK HOBBS AND HERBERT
SUTCLIFFE. Jack Hobbs of Surrey and
Herbert Sutcliffe of Yorkshire walking out to
bat at Scarborough during a Festival Match
versus New Zealand in 1931.

SURREY'S RECORD PAIR. Jack Hobbs
and Andy Sandham walking out to bat at
Lord's during a county championship
match versus Middlesex in 1930.

'THE MASTER' AT THE OVAL in 1926.

JACK HOBBS SURREY'S TOP SCORER. Jack Hobbs photographed at Harrods, Surrey's leading scorer of runs in first-class cricket.

PLAQUE COMMEMORATING JACK HOBBS WORLD RECORD Seen here is the plaque commemorating Jack Hobbs World Batting Record which he achieved during Somerset versus Surrey County Championship Match at the County Cricket Ground, Taunton on Saturday, Monday and Tuesday 15, 17 and 18 August 1925. The plaque still hangs in the Hobbs Room at the Oval today.

JACK HOBBS AT TAUNTON 1925. The actual run that gave 'The Master' his century that equalled Dr W.G. Grace's record of one hundred and twenty-five first-class centuries at Taunton for Surrey versus Somerset in 1925.

JACK HOBBS TAKING CONGRATULATIONS AT TAUNTON 1925. Jack Hobbs seen here taking congratulations from the Somerset players at the end of the over in which he scored his one hundred and twenty-fifth first-class century equalling Dr W.G. Grace's record at Taunton in 1925.

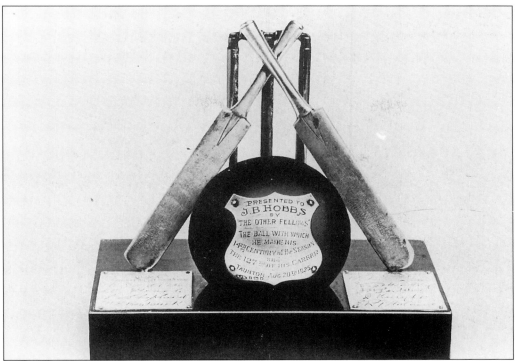

JACK HOBBS
MOMENTO FROM THE
SURREY PLAYERS.
Seen here is the momento
Jack Hobbs received from
the Surrey team on the
occasion that he surpassed
Dr W.G. Grace's record at
Taunton in 1925.

JACK HOBBS LETTER
FROM THE KING.
Illustrated here is a copy
of the letter Jack Hobbs
received from the King at
Balmoral Castle on 20
August 1925 after he had
exceeded the number of
centuries scored by Dr
W.G. Grace.

BALMORAL CASTLE.

20th. August, 1925.

Dear Mr. Hobbs,

The King has heard with much pleasure and
interest of your unique cricket achievement in
scoring 127 centuries, thus exceeding the number
made by the late Dr. W.G. Grace, and also attaining
a further record of 14 centuries in the course of
one season.

His Majesty warmly congratulates you upon
this remarkable success, whereby you have established
a new and greater record in the history of our
National Game.

Yours very truly,

J. Hobbs Esq.

Stamfordham

JACK HOBBS CENTURY OF CENTURIES. Depicted on a handkerchief produced in 1925 shortly after Jack Hobbs achieved this feat.

JACK HOBBS CENTURY OF CENTURIES PLATE. This plate celebrating Jack Hobbs, Hundred First-Class Hundreds was produced in 1980 by Nubern Products in recognition of the feat Jack Hobbs achieved in 1925.

JACK HOBBS AT THE CRICKET BAT SHOP 1920. Jack Hobbs at the premises of Messrs Summers Brown & Company of 40, Whitecross Street, London EC. Here Jack Hobbs was examining 'Force' cricket bats before they were sold. Jack Hobbs, in fact, had his own sports shop in Fleet Street from 1919 until his death. The shop continued in business until 1974 when it was moved to Islington High Street.

JACK HOBBS 'I ALWAYS USE WATERMANS'. This postcard was produced by the Watermans Pen Company and issued to would-be purchasers of the product. The postcard depicts Jack Hobbs smoking a cigarette and signing autographs for young collectors with what else, but a Watermans ink fountain pen. Many of these postcards, as this one, were signed by Jack Hobbs himself.

Lord's Ground.

MIDDLESEX v. SURREY.

SATURDAY, MONDAY & TUESDAY, AUGUST 28, 30, 31, 1926.

SURREY.	First Innings.	Second Innings.
1 Hobbs	not out 316	
2 Sandham	c Hendren, b Haig 58	
3 Ducat	b Durston 41	
4 Shepherd	c and b Stevens 15	
5 D. R. Jardine	c and b Powell 103	
6 A. Jeacocke	run out 26	
†7 P. G. H. Fender	not out 1	
8 E. R. T. Holmes		
9 Peach	Innings closed.	
*10 Strudwick		
11 Fenley, S.		
	B 12, l-b 7, w , n-b , 19	B , l-b , w , n-b ,
	Total 579	Total ......

FALL OF THE WICKETS.

1-115	2-216	3-258	4-528	5-575	6-	7-	8-	9-	10-
1-	2-	3-	4-	5-	6-	7-	8-	9-	10-

ANALYSIS OF BOWLING.

Name.	1st Innings.						2nd Innings.					
	O.	M.	R.	W.	Wd.	N-b.	O.	M.	R.	W.	Wd.	N-b
Haig	37	7	118	1	...	...	...	...	...	...	...	...
Durston	31	12	69	1	...	...	...	...	...	...	...	...
Allen	19	3	88	0	...	...	...	...	...	...	...	...
Stevens	22.3	1	95	1	...	...	...	...	...	...	...	...
Lee	8	1	44	0	...	...	...	...	...	...	...	...
Powell	27	4	109	1	...	...	...	...	...	...	...	...
Enthoven	10	1	37	0	...	...	...	...	...	...	...	...

MIDDLESEX.	First Innings.	Second Innings.
1 H. L. Dales	b Jardine 52	c Fender, b Holmes 4
2 G. T. S. Stevens	c Strudwick, b Holmes 2	c Fender, b Peach 63
3 G. O. Allen	c Shepherd, b Peach 21	c Jardine, b Fenley 17
4 Hendren, E.	not out 101	c Fenley, b Jardine 37
5 H. J. Enthoven	run out 1	b Fenley 5
†6 F. T. Mann	c Peach, b Jardine 3	not out 37
7 N. Haig	c Strudwick, b Fender ... 12	c Shepherd, b Fender ... 18
8 Lee, H. W.	run out 42	c Strudwick, b Holmes ... 31
9 Murrell	c Peach, b Fenley 20	c Fenley, b Peach 7
10 Durston	b Fender 0	b Holmes 1
11 Powell	c and b Fender 0	c Strudwick, b Holmes ... 4
	B 15, l-b 6, w , n-b , 21	B 11, l-b 3, w 2, n-b 1, 17
	Total 275	Total 241

FALL OF THE WICKETS.

1-2	2-37	3-112	4-120	5-125	5-147	7-240	9-275	9-275	10-275
1-5	2-31	3-115	4-122	5-156	6-188	7-209	8-224	9-229	10-241

ANALYSIS OF BOWLING.

Name.	1st Innings.						2nd Innings.					
	O.	M.	R.	W.	Wd.	N-b.	O.	M.	R.	W.	Wd.	N-b
Holmes	14	2	41	1	...	...	15.4	2	49	4	1	
Peach	18	7	26	1	...	...	23	5	41	2	...	
Fenley	24	4	76	1	...	...	23	4	66	2	...	
Fender	23	5	76	3	...	...	14	2	38	1	1	1
Shepherd	9	5	22	0	...	...	8	3	12	0	...	...
Jardine	8	2	13	2	...	...	6	1	18	1	...	...

Umpires—Burrows and Chidgey. Scorers—Burton and Boyington.

The figures on the Scoring Board show the Batsmen in.

Play Commences 1st day at 12, 2nd and 3rd day at 11.15

Luncheon at 1.30 p.m.   †Captain.   *Wicket-keeper.   Stumps drawn at 5.30 p.m.

SCORECARD MIDDLESEX VERSUS SURREY 1926. This is the original fully printed up scorecard of the Middlesex versus Surrey County Championship match Lord's Cricket Ground on Saturday, Monday and Tuesday 28, 30 and 31 August 1926 when Jack Hobbs achieved his highest score of 316 not out.

JACK HOBBS IN BUTTER 1923. Jack Hobbs sculptured in butter in the Australian pavilion at the British Empire Exhibition at Wembley in 1923. These exhibits were made of Australian butter and kept in a cooled cabinet under the title 'Australia wins the Test - in butter'.

JACK HOBBS OF ENGLAND.
Representing England in 61 Tests, Jack Hobbs scored 5,410 runs (av. 56.94) with a highest innings of 211 versus South Africa at Lord's in 1924. He also toured abroad seven times and can be seen here wearing his M.C.C. touring blazer and cap.

JACK HOBBS 'The Master'. A professional cricketer of the highest integrity Jack Hobbs also had a good sense of humour and he often had a laugh with his fellow cricketers especially during Festival Matches. He achieved the unique treble of scoring centuries for the Players versus Gentlemen in all three first-class fixtures of the 1919 season at the Oval, Lord's and Scarborough.

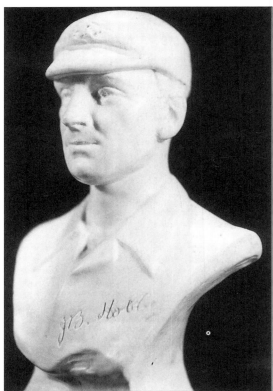

JACK HOBBS STATUE. A bust of Jack Hobbs produced for sale in 1925 the proceeds of which were to go towards the Middlesex Hospital rebuilding appeal.

JACK HOBBS WRITING FOR THE STAR 1932/33. This postcard was produced by *The Star* newspaper issued when Jack Hobbs went to Australia to report on the M.C.C. tour of Australia in 1932/33 which, thanks to his fellow Surrey colleague Douglas Jardine, will always be remembered as the 'Bodyline' series.

I want you to know—I am with the Test Team in Australia, describing the tour for "The Star"

JB. Hobbs,

JACK HOBBS WAITING TO BAT.

THE MASTER TAKING LUNCH. Sir Jack Hobbs, Harold Larwood and Herbert Sutcliffe taking Lunch. Today a traditional Lunch is celebrated on the birthday of the Sir Jack Hobbs,

the 16 December, each year at the Oval by members of The Masters Club. The menu is always roast lamb followed by apple pie and cream which was Sir Jack Hobbs' favourite meal.

JACK HOBBS rings the bell for play.

JACK HOBBS' LAST PUBLIC
APPEARANCE IN FLANNELS IN
1945.

Four

The Twenties, Thirties and Forties

SURREY TEAM 1929. Back row, left to right: R.J. Gregory, A. Ducat, T.F. Shepherd, E.R.T. Holmes, S. Fenley, H.A. Peach and A. Sandham. Front row, left to right: H. Strudwick, D.R. Jardine, P.G.H. Fender (captain), J.B. Hobbs and A. Jeacocke. The county was mid-table in the championship again, finishing tenth with 8 wins.

Hammett & Co., Printers, Parade, Taunton. **PRICE TWO PENCE.**

COUNTY CRICKET GROUND, TAUNTON.

Saturday, Monday and Tuesday, August 15th, 17th and 18th, 1925,

SOMERSET v. SURREY

FIRST INNINGS.	SOMERSET.	SECOND INNINGS.
1 J. C. W. MacBryan b Holmes ..	6	b Fender 109
2 Young c Sadler b Lockton	58	c Strudwick b Sadler 71
3 T. E. S. Francis b Sadler	0	c Strudwick b Lockton 12
4 J. C. White b Sadler	1	c Strudwick b Sadler 30
5 P. R. Johnson c & b Lockton	30	c Peach b Fender 16
6 E. F. Longrigg b Sadler	5	run out 4
7 R. A. Ingle b Fender	22	c Shepherd b Peach 23
8 Hunt b Lockton	4	b Fender 59
9 J. Bridges c & b Shepherd	25	b Fender 26
10 R. G. R.-Glasgow c Jardine b Lockton	4	c Sadler b Fender 5
11 M. Ll.-Hill not out	0	not out 1
b, 1-b8, n-b, w4 ..	12	b9, 1-b5, n-b4, w .. 18

Total ..167   Total ..374

1-11   2-12   3-16   4-93   5-110   6-112   7-118   8-126   9-163   10-167
1-184   2-203   3-228   4-262   5-268   6-268   7-310   8-352   9-373   10-374

FIRST INNINGS.	SURREY.	SECOND INNINGS.
1 Hobbs c Hill b Bridges	101	not out 101
2 Sandham c Longrigg b Bridges ..	13	not out 74
3 D. J. Knight run out	34	....
4 Shepherd b White	0	....
5 D. R. Jardine run out	47	....
6 E. R. T. Holmes c Hill b Glasgow ..	24	....
7 P. G. H. Fender st. Hill b Young ..	59	....
8 Peach b Young	20	....
9 J. H. Lockton absent		....
10 Sadler c Johnson b Young	25	....
11 Strudwick not out	10	....
b15, 1-b8, n-b3, w ..	26	b6, 1-b1, n-b1, w .. 8

Total .. 359   Total ..183

1-50   2-146   3-148   4-170   5-221   6-260   7-322   8-325   9-359   10-
1-   2-   3-   4-   5-   6-   7-   8-   9-   10-

Scorers—Trump & Boyington.   Umpires—Draper & Young.

Lunch Interval 1.30 p.m.   Tea Interval 4.15 p.m.   Stumps Drawn 5.30 p.m.

SCORECARD SOMERSET VERSUS SURREY 1925. The original fully printed up scorecard of the Somerset versus Surrey County Championship Match at the County Cricket Ground, Taunton on Saturday, Monday and Tuesday 15, 17 and 18 August, 1925 when Jack Hobbs achieved his record of one hundred first-class centuries.

JACK HOBBS TAKING TO THE
FIELD WITH ANDY SANDHAM.

JACK HOBBS AND HERBERT
SUTCLIFFE. Jack Hobbs of Surrey and
Herbert Sutcliffe of Yorkshire walking out to
bat at Scarborough during a Festival Match in
1932.

SURREY TEAM 1922. Back row, left to right: A. Ducat, A.C.T. Geary, W.J. Abel, T.F. Shepherd, A. Sandham and H.A. Peach. Front row, left to right: J.W. Hitch, J.B. Hobbs, P.G.H. Fender (captain), A. Jeacocke and H. Strudwick. Thanks to 13 wins, 10 draws and just a single defeat, Percy Fender guided the county to third in the championship.

JACK HOBBS AND ANDY SANDHAM. Jack Hobbs and Andy Sandham walking out to bat at Blackheath during a county championship match versus Kent in 1922.

Surrey County Cricket Club 2d.

KENNINGTON OVAL
SURREY v. NEW ZEALAND
WEDNESDAY, AUGUST 3rd, 1927   (Three-Day Match)

NEW ZEALAND

		First Innings		Second Innings	
1	C. S. Dempster	c Holmes, b Geary	6	c Peach, b Geary	101
2	J. E. Mills	c Machin, b Peach	103	b Holmes	23
3	R. C. Blunt	c Barling, b Peach	54	c Geary b Shepherd	36
4	M. L. Page	c Barling, b McCanlis	66	c Machin, b Geary	68
5	C. W. Allcott	b Geary	13	c Machin b Shepherd	0
* 6	T. C. Lowry	c Machin, b Peach	20	c McCanlis, b Peach	4
7	C. C. Dacre	c Machin, b Peach	8	b McCanlis	19
8	H. M. McGirr	c Shepherd, b Geary	3	c Machin b Peach	66
9	W. E. Merritt	c Machin, b Holmes	7	c Sandham b Geary	39
†10	K. C. James	not out	12	c Sandham, b Geary	3
11	M. Henderson	c Shepherd, b Holmes	0	Not out	5
		B 13, l-b 8, w , n-b	21	B 2, l-b 9, w , n-b 2	13
		Total	313	Total	371

FALL OF THE WICKETS

1-8	2-152	3-226	4-254	5-277	6-285	7-294	8-296	9-313
1-52	2-197	3-204	4-208	5-218	6-275	7-295	8-296	9-352

BOWLING ANALYSIS

	1st Innings					2nd Innings				
	O.	M.	R.	W.	Wd. N-b.	O.	M.	R.	W.	Wd. N-b.
Geary	29	6	61	3	...					
McCanlis	16	4	41	1	...					
Peach	29	5	78	4	...					
Holmes	11	0	35	2	...					
Shepherd	19	3	45	0	...					
Gregory	10	4	32	0	...					

SURREY

		First Innings		Second Innings	
1	Hobbs	c Dacre, b Blunt	146	c Merritt b McGirr	0
2	Sandham	b Dempster	66	c James b Merritt	50
3	Ducat	b Blunt	32	c Blunt b Allcott	100
4	Shepherd	lbw, b Blunt	29	st James b Merritt	3
5	Barling	lbw, b Blunt	18	Not out	78
* 6	E. R. T. Holmes	st James, b McGirr	13	st James b Merritt	23
8	Gregory	st James, b Merritt	18	lbw b Merritt	8
9	Peach	c Allcott, b Merritt	30	b Merritt	8
†11	R. S. Machin	c Page, b Dempster	1	b Blunt	2
7	M. A. McCanlis	st James, b Merritt	11	Not out	19
10	Geary (A.)	not out	0		
		B 11, l-b 2, w , n-b	13	B 3, l-b 3, w , n-b	6
		Total	377	Total for 8	284

FALL OF THE WICKETS

1-180	2-241	3-281	4-292	5-307	6-325	7-347	8-356	9-370
1-0	2-105	3-121	4-167	5-167	6-191	7-	8-	9-

BOWLING ANALYSIS

	1st Innings					2nd Innings				
	O.	M.	R.	W.	Wd. N-b.	O.	M.	R.	W.	Wd. N-b.
McGirr	13	1	43	1	...					
Henderson	12	6	22	0	...					
Blunt	28	3	128	4	...					
Merritt	23.3	3	106	3	...					
Allcott	9	3	30	0	...					
Lowry	4	0	16	0	...					
Dempster	5	1	19	2	...					

* Captain.
† Wkt.-keeper.
Umpires—Cuffe and Day.

Toss won by New Zealand.
Hours of Play and Intervals—see back.
RESULT— DRAWN

SCORECARD SURREY VERSUS NEW ZEALANDERS 1927. This is the original fully printed up scorecard of the Surrey versus New Zealanders tour match at the Oval on Wednesday 3rd August 1927.

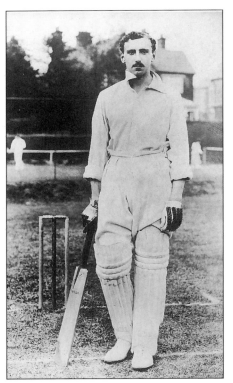

PERCY FENDER. Born at Balham, London in 1892, Percy Fender was an exceptional right-handed all-rounder who represented Sussex between 1910 and 1913 before joining Surrey in 1914 where he later captained the county between 1921 and 1931. With features that made him a cartoonist's delight he made cricket history scoring a century in just 35 minutes for Surrey versus Northamptonshire at the county ground, Northampton in 1920. Representing Surrey in 414 first-class matches, he scored 14,117 runs (av. 28.00) with 17 centuries and a top score of 185. He also took 1,586 wickets (av. 24.08) with a best of 8 for 24 and he held 470 catches. In 1921 he became the first player to achieve the treble and on six occasions accomplished the double. He played 13 Tests for England scoring 380 runs (av. 19.00), took 29 wickets (av. 40.86) and he toured abroad on three occasions. Away from cricket, he kept goal for the Corinthian Casuals and Fulham and as a cricket writer and journalist he wrote four cricket books. On his retirement he joined a family owned wine business. He died at Exeter in 1985.

THE TWELFTH MAN. Percy Fender was the cartoonists' delight and here is a cartoon of Percy Fender, drawn by the famous Australian cricketer Arthur Mailey.

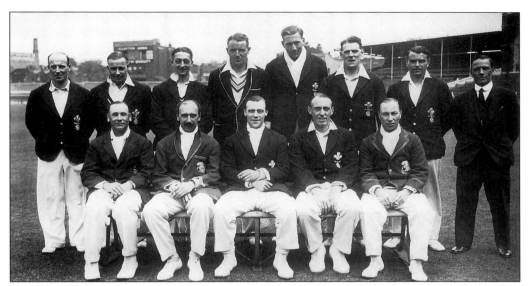

SURREY TEAM 1934. Back row, left to right: R.J. Gregory, T.H. Barling, H.S. Squires, E.A. Watts, A.R. Gover, E.W.J. Brooks, E.F. Wilson and H. Strudwick (scorer). Front row, left to right: J.B. Hobbs, P.G.H. Fender, E.R.T. Holmes (captain), H.M. Garland-Wells (vice-captain) and A. Sandham. The county finished the season eleventh in the county championship and the end of the season saw the retirement from county cricket of Jack Hobbs.

ANDREW DUCAT. Born at Brixton, London in 1886, Andy Ducat the cricketer, was a sound right-handed middle order batsman and slow right-arm bowler. He represented Surrey from 1906 to 1931 in 422 first-class matches, scoring 23,108 runs (av. 38.64) with 52 centuries. He scored eight double centuries for the county of which his highest score was 306 not out versus Oxford University at the Oval in 1919 and he held 202 catches. He hit 1,000 runs in a season on fourteen occasions, with his best season being 1930 when he achieved 2,067 runs (av. 49.21). Representing England in only one Test Match in 1921 he also toured Australia in 1929/30 in emergency but did not play a Test. He died at Lord's cricket ground on July 23rd, 1942 of heart failure whilst batting.

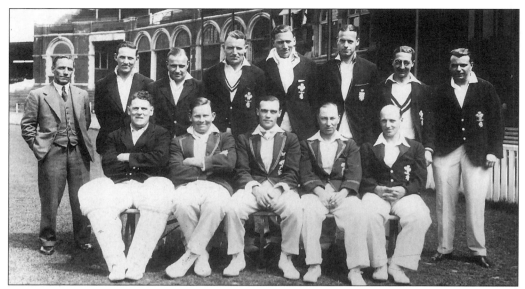

SURREY TEAM 1936. Back row, left to right: H. Strudwick (scorer), L.B. Fishlock, T.H. Barling, E.A. Watts, A.R. Gover, J.F. Parker, H.S. Squires and E.F. Wilson. Front row, left to right: E.W.J. Brooks, F.R. Brown, E.R.T. Holmes (captain), A. Sandham and R.J. Gregory. Errol Holmes in his third season as county captain led the county to sixth in the county championship with 9 victories.

JACK HOBBS AND DULEEPSINHJI. Jack Hobbs of Surrey and Duleepsinhji of Sussex walking out to bat at Scarborough during a Festival Match in 1933.

JACK HOBBS AND WILLIAM
WHYSALL. Jack Hobbs of Surrey and
William Whysall of Nottinghamshire walking
out to bat at Scarborough during a Festival
Match in 1926.

DOUGLAS JARDINE. Born at Bombay,
India in 1900 while his Scottish father was
Advocate-General of Bombay, Douglas
Jardine learnt his cricket at Winchester
before gaining three Oxford Blues between
1920 and 1923. Normally sporting the
Harlequin Club cap he was a forceful right-
handed batsman, reliable leg-break bowler
and handy fieldsman. Representing Surrey
between 1921 and 1933 he played 141 first-
class matches, scoring 7,037 runs (av.
44.53) with 14 centuries and a top score of
167. He also took 25 wickets (av. 36.64)
and he held 102 catches. Playing 22 Tests
for England, he captained his country
fifteen times with nine victories being
without doubt the most controversial Test
captain having devised the 'bodyline' tactics
in Australia in 1932/33 to reduce Don
Bradman's run making. In Tests he scored
1,296 runs (av. 48.00) with a top score of
127 versus the West Indies at Old Trafford,
Manchester in 1933. He was by profession a
solicitor and he wrote four cricket books.
He contracted tick fever in Southern
Rhodesia and later died at Montreux,
Switzerland in 1958.

ERROL HOLMES AND BILL BOWES. Errol Holmes of Surrey and Bill Bowes of Yorkshire viewing the cricket at Scarborough during a Festival Match in 1936.

LAURIE FISHLOCK AND GERALD MOBEY. Surrey opening pair, Laurie Fishlock (left) and Gerald Mobey, on the way to the wicket during the Trial Match at the Oval on Saturday 27 April 1946 for N.H. Bennett's XI versus R.R. Blades' XI. A saturated pitch delayed the start and once at the wicket Gerald Mobey was bowled by Alec Bedser for 4 whilst Laurie Fishlock went on to score 50 before retiring.

THIS CARD DOES NOT NECESSARILY INCLUDE THE FALL OF THE LAST WICKET

Surrey County Cricket Club 2ᵈ·

KENNINGTON OVAL

SURREY v. YORKSHIRE

SATURDAY, AUGUST 20th, 1932. (Three-Day Match)

	SURREY	First Innings		Second Innings	
1	Hobbs	c Wood, b Macaulay	90	c Wood b Bowes	1.
2	Sandham	c Wood, b Macaulay	9	b Bowes	11.
3	Gregory	c Mitchell, b Bowes	11	c Hall b Bowes	2.
4	S. A. Block	b Fisher	0	c Hall b Macaulay	9.
*5	D. R. Jardine	b Leyland	35	lbw b. Fisher	29.
6	F. R. Brown	b Verity	14	b Bowes	3.
7	Whitfield	not out	10	c Fisher b Bowes	19.
8	P. G. H. Fender	b Verity	21	b Fisher	7.
9	M. J. C. Allom	b Bowes	21	c Macaulay b Verity	10
10	Parker	c Macaulay, b Bowes	2	b Bowes	7.
‡11	Brooks	b Bowes	0	Not out	15
		B 12, l-b 4, w , n-b 2	18	B 2, l-b 2 w , n-b 1	5
		Total	231	Total	118.

FALL OF THE WICKETS

1–31	2–60	3–60	4–135	5–164	6–188	7–194	8–225	9–230	10–231
1–	2–	3–	4–	5–	6–	7–	8–	9–	10–

BOWLING ANALYSIS

	1st Innings					2nd Innings				
	O.	M.	R.	W.	Wd. N-b.	O.	M.	R.	W.	Wd. N-b.
Bowes	28.3	3	86	4	2	29.5	9	49	6	
Macaulay	19	7	23	2		14	6	16	1	
Hall	8	0	32	0		4	1	8	0	
Fisher	28	13	38	1		6	4	11	2	
Verity	11	4	20	2		21	10	29	1	
Leyland	4	0	14	1						

	YORKSHIRE	First Innings		Second Innings	
4	Mitchell	c Fender, b Allom	12	c Brooks b Fender	12
8	Verity	c Fender, b Allom	22	lbw b Brown	9
1	Sutcliffe	c Brooks, b Brown	4	Run out	6
2	Barber	c Brown, b Allom	32	c Parker b Allom	18
3	Leyland	c Hobbs, b Allom	37	b Fender	34
*7	A. B. Sellers	st Brooks b Parker	8	b Fender	18
6	Fisher	c Gregory b Allom	22	c Brooks b Brown	5
‡9	Wood	Not out	29	Not out	17
5	Macaulay	c Brooks b Allom	0	Not out	2
11	Bowes	c Brown b Fender	7		
10	Hall	lbw b Fender	8		
		B 20, l-b 8, w 3, n-b 3	34	B 11, l-b 2, w , n-b 1	14
		Total	215	Total For 7 wkts.	135

FALL OF THE WICKETS

1–41	2–46	3–52	4–107	5–119	6–	7–	8–	9–	10–
1–	2–	3–	4–	5–	6–	7–	8–	9–	10–

BOWLING ANALYSIS

	1st Innings					2nd Innings				
	O.	M.	R.	W.	Wd. N-b.	O.	M.	R.	W.	Wd. N-b.
M. J. C. Allom	31	12	75	6		11	5	21	1	
J. F. Parker	9	1	31	1		9	2	25	0	
F. R. Brown	29	14	45	1		20	6	43	2	
P. G. H. Fender	19.2	9	26	2		14.2	3	32	3	
R. J. Gregory	2	1	4	0						

* Captain.
‡ Wkt.-keeper.
Umpires—Hendren & Chester

Toss won by SURREY
Hours of Play—see back
RESULT— Yorkshire won by 3 wickets.

SCORECARD SURREY VERSUS YORKSHIRE 1932. This is the original fully printed up scorecard of the Surrey versus Yorkshire match at the Oval on Saturday 20 August 1932, day one of a three day match.

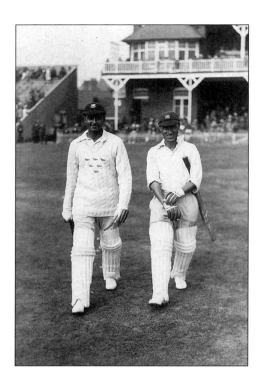

DULEEPSINHJI AND ANDY SANDHAM.
Duleepsinhji of Sussex and Andy Sandham of
Surrey walking out to bat at Scarborough during
a Festival Match in 1933.

ERROL HOLMES AND HIS SIDE 1937. Errol Holmes the Surrey captain discusses tactics
with the score at 91 for 6 as the scoreboard above him shows against Sussex at Hastings.

SURREY TEAM 1946. Back row, left to right: H. Strudwick (scorer), E.A. Watts, G.J. Whittaker, L.B. Fishlock, G.S. Mobey, J.F. Parker, E.A. Bedser, A.V. Bedser, A.R. Gover and J. Tait (masseur). Front row, left to right: T.H. Barling, N.H. Bennett (captain), R.J. Gregory and H.S. Squires. The first season after the end of the Second World War saw Nigel Bennett in his only season as skipper guide Surrey to eleventh in the county championship with just 6 wins.

HARRY SQUIRES. Born at Kingston-upon-Thames, Surrey in 1909, Harry Squires was a stylish middle order right-handed batsman and right-arm medium pace off-break or leg-break bowler. He represented the county in 402 first-class matches, scoring 18,636 runs (av. 31.11) with 36 hundreds including a top score of 236 versus Lancashire at the Oval in 1933. He also took 297 wickets (av. 35.34) with a best of 8 for 52 and he held 137 catches. He achieved 1,000 runs in a season eleven times and his best season was 1947 when he amassed 1,847 runs (av. 36.94). He was appointed county secretary and died at Old Deer Park, Richmond in 1950 following a short illness from a virus.

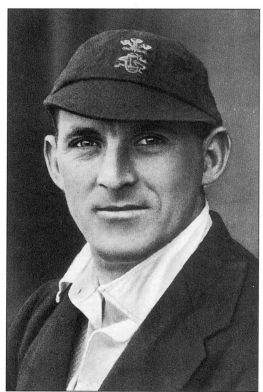

LAURIE FISHLOCK. Born at Battersea, London in 1907, Laurie Fishlock was a dashing left-handed opening batsman and slow-left arm bowler. He represented Surrey in 347 first-class matches from 1931 to 1952, scoring 22,138 runs (av. 40.47) with 50 centuries including a highest score of 253 versus Leicestershire at Leicester in 1948 and he took 9 wickets (av. 48.11) with a best of 4 for 62 and he held 187 catches. He achieved 1,000 runs in a season twelve times and went onto exceed 2,000 runs in a season six times. His best season was in 1949 when he amassed 2,426 runs (av. 45.77). Playing 4 Tests for England between 1936 and 1946/47 he had little success although he toured Australia and New Zealand twice in 1936/37 and 1946/47. A regular soccer player at outside-left he appeared for Crystal Palace, Millwall, Aldershot, Southampton, Gillingham and also was capped once as an amateur international for England. He died at Sutton, Surrey in 1986.

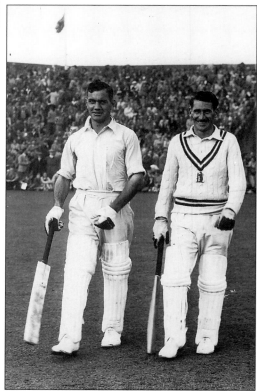

ALEC BEDSER AND TOM PRITCHARD. Alec Bedser of Surrey and Tom Pritchard of Warwickshire walking out to bat at Scarborough during a Festival Match in 1948.

SURREY COUNTY C.C.

SURREY TEAM 1935. Back row, left to right:
G.J. Whittaker, L.B. Fishlock, E.A. Watts,
A.R. Gover, J.F. Parker, H.S. Squires and
K.C.W. King. Middle row, left to right:
R.J. Gregory, A. Sandham, E.R.T. Holmes
(captain), E.W.J. Brooks and T.H. Barling.
Front row, left to right: H. Strudwick (scorer).
The first season without the illustrious 'Master'
Jack Hobbs, the county again finished eleventh
in the county championship as they had in 1934
with 7 wins.

DONALD KNIGHT. Born at Sutton, Surrey in
1894 Donald Knight was a stylish right-handed
opening batsman and good close fieldsman.
Learning his cricket at Malvern where he was
captain in 1912-13, he also captained the Public
Schools XI at Lord's and like Miles Howell
obtained Blues at Oxford in 1914 and 1919. He
represented Surrey from 1911 to 1937 playing
107 first-class matches and accumulating 4,390
runs (av. 29.66) with 9 centuries and a highest
score of 146. Although being in the scholastic
profession, which limited his appearances for
the county after leaving university, his best
season was 1919 when he achieved 1,588 runs
(av. 45.37). He represented England in two
Tests in 1921 with a top score of 38 and he died
at Marylebone, London in 1960.

Surrey County Cricket Club

KENNINGTON OVAL

SURREY v. WEST INDIES

WEDNESDAY, JULY 26th, 1939 (Three-Day Match)

WEST INDIES		First Innings	Second Innings
1 V. Stollmeyer	Trinidad		
2 J. Stollmeyer	Trinidad	c Dickinson, b Gover...... 6	
3 G. Headley	Jamaica		
4 G. Gomez	Trinidad		
5 K. H. Weekes	Jamaica		
‡6 I. Barrow	Jamaica		
*7 R. S. Grant	Trinidad		
8 L. N. Constantine	Trinidad		
9 E. A. Martindale	Barbados		
10 C. B. Clarke	Barbados		
11 T. Johnson	Trinidad		

B , l-b , w , n-b ......   B , l-b , w , n-b ......

Total..........   Total..........

FALL OF THE WICKETS

| 1-19 | 2- | 3- | 4- | 5- | 6- | 7- | 8- | 9- | 10- |
| 1- | 2- | 3- | 4- | 5- | 6- | 7- | 8- | 9- | 10- |

BOWLING ANALYSIS   First Innings   Second Innings

O.   M.   R.   W.   Wd.   N.b.   O.   M.   R.   W.   Wd.   N.b.

SURREY	First Innings	Second Innings
1 Gregory		
2 Fishlock		
3 Whitfield		
4 Squires		
5 Parker		
6 P. J. Dickinson		
*7 H. M. Garland Wells		
‡8 Mobey		
9 Constable		
10 Watts		
11 Gover		

B , l-b , w , n-b ......   B , l-b , w , n-b ......

Total..........   Total..........

FALL OF THE WICKETS

| 1- | 2- | 3- | 4- | 5- | 6- | 7- | 8- | 9- | 10- |
| 1- | 2- | 3- | 4- | 5- | 6- | 7- | 8- | 9- | 10- |

BOWLING ANALYSIS   First Innings   Second Innings

O.   M.   R.   W.   Wd.   N.b   O.   M.   R.   W.   Wd.   N.b.

*Captain   ‡Wkt.-keeper   Toss won by WEST INDIES

Umpires—Lee (G.M.) & Chester   RESULT—

HOURS OF PLAY : 1st & 2nd DAYS 11.30—6.30 LUNCH 1.30   3rd DAY 11.30—4.0 or 6.30 LUNCH 1.30

Printed on the Ground by the Surrey County Cricket Club Printing Department

SCORECARD SOMERSET VERSUS WEST INDIES 1939. The original first day printed up scorecard of the Surrey versus touring West Indians at the Oval on Wednesday 26 July 1939. West Indies beat Surrey by 7 wickets in this match thanks to Bertie Clarke who was responsible for taking the last five Surrey wickets for just 22 runs, so helping the tourists to victory a quarter of an hour from time on the final day. West Indies (487 and 49 for 3) beat Surrey (274 and 261) by 7 wickets.

ERROL HOLMES. Born at Calcutta, India in 1905 Errol Holmes was a hard-hitting right-handed middle order batsman and right-arm fast-medium bowler. Learning his cricket at Malvern he graduated to Oxford University where he obtained Blues all three years between 1925-27 and also achieved a Blue at soccer as a freshman in 1925. While at Oxford during his season as captain, he made a career best 236 for the university versus the Free Foresters at the Parks in 1927. He represented the county between 1924 and 1955 in 198 first-class matches, scoring 8,837 runs (av. 34.25) with 15 centuries and a top score of 206 versus Derbyshire at Chesterfield in 1935, he also took 173 wickets (av. 35.46) with a best of 6 for 16 and he held 145 catches mainly at short slip. He achieved 1,000 runs in a season six times and his best season was 1935 when he amassed 1,925 runs (av. 41.84). Playing little or no cricket from 1928 to 1933 he returned to captain the county from 1934 to 1938 with a second spell in 1947-48. He represented England in five Tests between 1934/35 and 1935 and led the M.C.C. to Australia and New Zealand in 1935/36. He toured abroad three times and died of a heart attack at Marylebone, London in 1960.

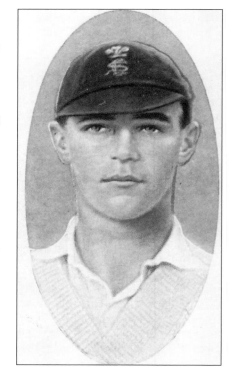

Five
The Kennington Oval

THE OVAL 1848. The Surrey Cricket Ground at the Oval in 1848, from a print published in 1848 by Ackermann & Company of London.

THE OVAL c. 1850. A member of the Walworth club, Mr William Baker, came to the assistance of the Surrey County Cricket Club when he suggested that Kennington Oval, a market garden and the property of the Duchy of Cornwall, might be used for cricket. The Duchy was willing to let it for the purpose of a cricket ground and a lease of 31 years was granted at £120 per year, with taxes which amounted to a further £20. At the time of its conversion to a cricket ground, Kennington Oval was mainly an open space with a small hedge surrounding it and the ground takes its name from the surrounding streets rather than the shape of the playing area itself. The original turf came from Tooting Common and was laid in March 1845 by Mr M. Turtle of Clapham Road for £300. This photograph of the ground c. 1850 shows a view from the Vauxhall End looking towards the pavilion.

THE OVAL 1880. A view of the Oval during the match between England and Australia on September 6, 7 and 8, 1880.

FLOODLIT FOOTBALL AT THE OVAL. Floodlit football at the Oval during the time Charles Alcock was establishing the ground for F.A. Cup Finals and England international matches. England played Scotland at the Oval in 1873, 1875, 1877, 1879, 1881, 1885 and 1889 and England hosted Wales at the Oval in 1879, 1883, 1887. Other matches followed including North versus South 1879/80, 1881/82, 1883/84, 1885/86, 1887/88 and 1889/90, Oxford University versus Cambridge University 1873/74 to 1886/87, London versus Sheffield 1872 to 1890 London versus Oxford and Cambridge 1881/82 to 1891/92. Rugby Union internationals were also staged at the Oval by England versus Scotland in 1872 to 1878 and versus Ireland in 1875 to 1879, North versus South in 1874/75 to 1880/81 and Oxford University versus Cambridge University in 1873/74 to 1879/80.

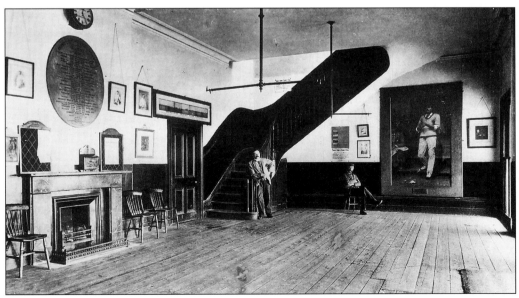

THE LONG ROOM AT THE OVAL. A view of the Pavilion Long Room in 1900.

THE OVAL 1902. A view of the pavilion, east and west stands.

THE OVAL 1904. A view of the Vauxhall End of the ground as it was in 1904 taken from the first floor of the pavilion with a county match in progress.

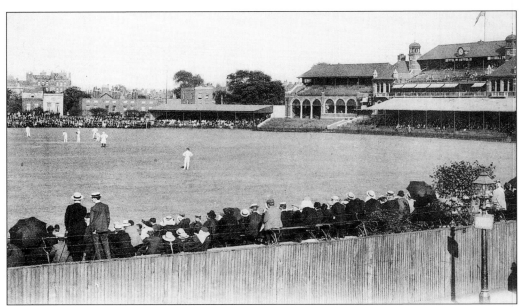

THE OVAL 1905. A view of the pavilion and east stand taken from Kennington Oval with a match in progress and a huge crowd observing cricket during the 1905 season.

THE OVAL 1912. The first match on at Kennington Oval was recorded as having been played in May 1845 between Mr Fould's XI and Mr Houghton's XI. The first Surrey match was in August 1845 between the Gentlemen of Surrey and the Players of Surrey. Following the meeting of the Montpelier Club in August 1845 at the Horns Tavern, Kennington, more than one hundred members of different local cricket clubs in the county proposed the formation of the County Club for the County of Surrey. The resolution was carried amidst cheering and the formal inauguration took place at the Horns Tavern in October 1845. The first Surrey County Cricket Club home match was staged with neighbours, Kent in 1846 while the first county championship fixture was staged versus Sussex in 1873 with the first Test Match in 1880 between England and Australia. This view of the ground was taken during the Surrey versus South Africans tourists match.

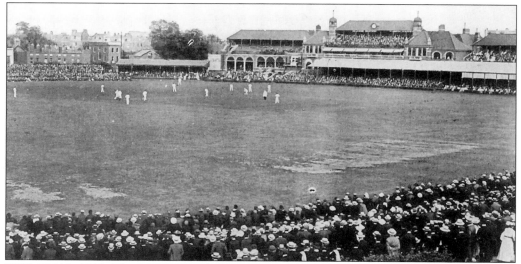

THE OVAL 1919. The current pavilion was built in 1896 and was designed by the architect Mr A.T. Muirhead who was also responsible for the design of the Old Trafford pavilion at Manchester. This view of the pavilion shows play in progress during the 1919 season, from the Vauxhall End looking towards the pavilion, nets and west stand.

A VIEW OF THE OVAL IN 1930.

THE OVAL 1953. This a view of the ground in 1953 and it is clear from this picture the ground is very much located in an urban situation, overshadowed as it has been for so many years by the gas holders and blocks of flats, but still retaining from the upper part of the pavilion a fine view of the tower of the Palace of Westminster and central London.

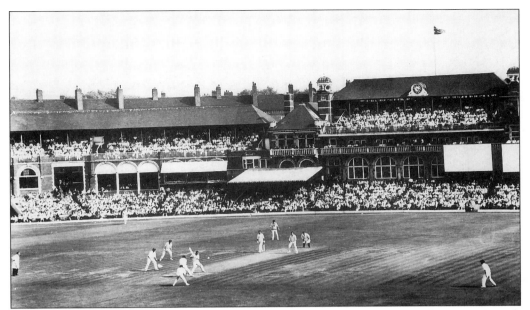

THE OVAL PAVILION 1963. This a view of the ground and Pavilion was taken in 1963 with play in progress. Crowds at the Oval were usually around 10,000 to 12,000 for county and Test matches, but the largest attendance over three days to attend a match at the ground was 80,000 for the Surrey versus Yorkshire County Championship match in 1906, when many spectators were required to stand all day.

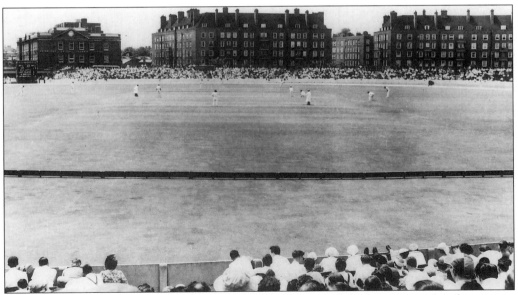

THE OVAL 1965. This view of the ground is from the East side looking across the playing area towards the Archbishop Tennisons Grammar School and some of the many flats which surround the Oval.

THE HOBBS GATES AT THE OVAL. Here are the Hobbs Gates which were built in honour of the great Surrey and England cricketer.

Six

The Kingston Festival, the Fifties and Beyond

SURREY TEAM 1951. Back row, left to right: B. Constable, D.G.W. Fletcher, J.W. McMahon, J.C. Laker, E.A. Bedser, G.A.R. Lock, G.J. Whittaker and A.J. McIntyre (wkt-kpr.) Front row, left to right: J.F. Parker, W.S. Surridge, M.R. Barton (captain), L.B. Fishlock and A.V. Bedser. The county finished 6th in the county championship in 1951 winning 7, drawing 15 and losing 6 championship matches.

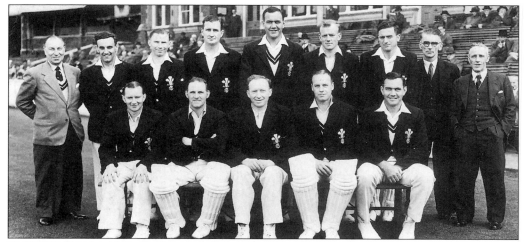

SURREY TEAM 1952. Back row, left to right: A. Sandham (coach), B. Constable, D.G.W. Fletcher, J.C. Laker, E.A. Bedser, G.A.R. Lock, G.J. Whittaker, J Tait (masseur) and H. Strudwick (scorer). Front row, left to right: A.J. McIntyre (wkt-kpr.), L.B. Fishlock, W.S. Surridge (captain), J.F. Parker and A.V. Bedser. The year 1952 was the first of seven consecutive county championship victories for the county under the leadership of Stuart Surridge. Of the 28 championship matches 20 were won.

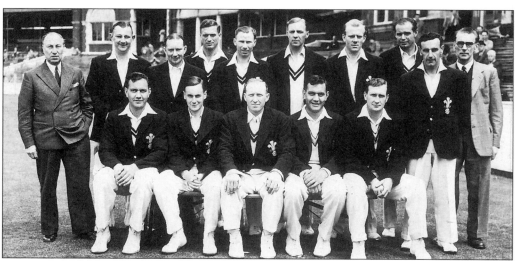

SURREY TEAM 1953. Back row, left to right: A. Sandham (coach), G.N.G. Kirby, A.J. McIntyre (wkt-kpr.), G.J. Whittaker, D.G.W. Fletcher, T.H. Clark, G.A.R. Lock, J.W. McMahon and J. Tait (masseur). Front row, left to right: E.A. Bedser, P.B.H. May, W.S. Surridge (captain), A.V. Bedser, J.C. Laker and B. Constable. Champions again in 1953 although only 13 matches were won.

SURREY TEAM 1954. Back row, left to right: A. Sandham (coach), P.J. Loader, R. Subba Row, E.A. Bedser, G.A.R. Lock, T.H. Clark, J.C. Laker, H. Strudwick (scorer) and J. Tait (masseur). Front row, left to right: B. Constable, A.J. McIntyre (wkt-kpr.), P.B.H. May, W.S. Surridge (captain), A.V. Bedser and D.G.W. Fletcher. Champions again under the leadership of Stuart Surridge with 15 victories.

SURREY TEAM 1955. Back row, left to right: H. Strudwick (scorer), B. Constable, P.J. Loader, T.H. Clark, G.A.R. Lock, E.A. Bedser, D.G.W. Fletcher, J.C. Laker, R.C.E. Pratt, J. Tait (masseur) and A. Sandham (coach). Front row, left to right: M.J. Stewart, A.J. McIntyre (wkt-kpr.), P.B.H. May, W.S. Surridge (captain), A.V. Bedser and K.F. Barrington. Champions with a record 23 victories.

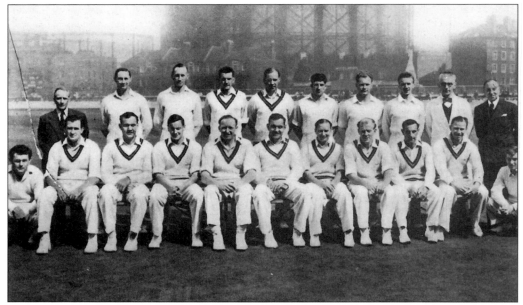

SURREY TEAM 1956. Back row, left to right: H. Strudwick (scorer), R. E.C. Pratt, D.E. Pratt, P.J. Loader, T.H. Clark, K.F. Barrington, D.F. Cox, M.J. Stewart, J. Tait (masseur) and A. Sandham (coach). Front row, left to right: A.F. Brazier, J.C. Laker, E.A. Bedser, P.B.H. May, W.S. Surridge (captain), A.V. Bedser, A.J. McIntyre (wkt-kpr.), G.A.R. Lock, B. Constable, D.G.W. Fletcher and R. Swetman. County champions yet again with 15 victories in Stuart Surridge's last season as skipper.

SURREY TEAM 1957. Back row, left to right: H. Strudwick (scorer), K.F. Barrington, D.E. Pratt, D.G.W. Fletcher, T.H. Clark, P.J. Loader, M.J. Stewart, G.A.R. Lock, R.C.E. Pratt, B. Constable, J. Tait (masseur) and A. Sandham (coach). Front row, left to right: D.F. Cox, E.A. Bedser, A.V. Bedser (vice-captain), P.B.H. May (captain), A.J. McIntyre (wkt-kpr.), J.C. Laker and R. Swetman. Under the new captain Peter May the county again celebrated the season as county champions with 21 victories and only 3 defeats.

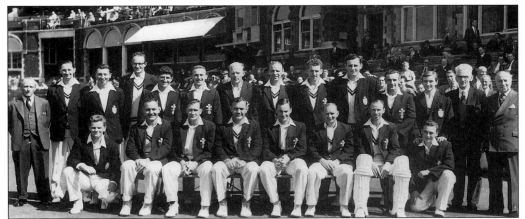

SURREY TEAM 1958. Back row, left to right: H. Strudwick (scorer), R.C.E. Pratt, M.D. Willett, J.K. Hall, K.F. Barrington, M.J. Stewart, G.A.R. Lock, T.H. Clark, P.J. Loader, D. Gibson, B. Constable, R. Swetman, J. Tait (masseur) and A. Sandham (coach). Front row, left to right: D. Sydenham, E.A. Bedser, J.C. Laker, A.V. Bedser (vice-captain), P.B.H. May (captain), A.J. McIntyre (wkt-kpr.), D.G.W. Fletcher and A.B.D. Parsons. The last of the 7 consecutive championship winning seasons and the last until 1971.

KINGSTON-ON-THAMES CRICKET FESTIVAL SOUTH TEAM 1948. Back row, left to right: G.S. Mobey (umpire), S.M. Brown, T.P.B. Smith, L. Gray, R.R. Dovey, S.S. Surridge, A.J. McIntyre and S.H. Hipple (umpire). Front row, left to right: H.S. Squires, J. Sims, M.R. Barton, L.J. Todd and L.B. Fishlock.

KINGSTON-ON-THAMES CRICKET FESTIVAL EAST TEAM 1948. Back row, left to right: G.S. Mobey (umpire), S.M. Brown, R. Smith, L. Gray, T.C. Dodds, R.R. Dovey, S.H. Hipple (umpire). Front row, left to right: R. Smith, J. Sims, H.A. Pawson, L.J. Todd, T.H. Barling and A.J. McIntyre.

KINGSTON-ON-THAMES CRICKET FESTIVAL NORTH TEAM 1948. Back row, left to right: G.S. Mobey (umpire), B. Constable, N. Oldfield, A.E.G. Rhodes, J.V. Wilson, R.W. Clarke, W. Place, S.H. Hipple (umpire). Front row, left to right: P. Corrall, J.E. Walsh, W.A. Sime, D. Brookes and A.E. Nutter.

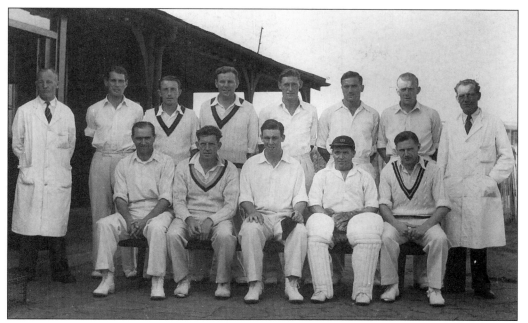

KINGSTON-ON-THAMES CRICKET FESTIVAL NORTH TEAM 1949. Back row, left to right: G.S. Mobey (umpire), J.T. Ikin, G.A. Edrich, W.B. Roberts, G.J. Whittaker, M. Tompkin, G.A.R. Lock W.F. Price (umpire). Front row, left to right: D. Brookes, W.H. Copson, N.D. Howard, H. Yarnold and A.E. Nutter.

KINGSTON-ON-THAMES CRICKET FESTIVAL COMMONWEALTH TEAM 1950. Back row, left to right: K. McCanlis (umpire), P.R. Umrigar, A.H. Kardar, Khan Mohammad, D. Fitzmaurice, T.L. Pritchard, B.H. Pairaudeau, G.S. Mobey (umpire). Front row, left to right: V.S. Hazare, L. Livingstone, B.A. Barnett, V. Mankad and K. Grieves.

KINGSTON-ON-THAMES CRICKET FESTIVAL NORTH TEAM 1950. Back row, left to right: K. McCanlis (umpire), G. Dawkes, R. Tattersall, N. Oldfield, R. Berry, A.E.G. Rhodes, K. Grieves G.S. Mobey (umpire). Front row, left to right: L. Livingstone, D. Brookes, N.D. Howard, T.L. Pritchard and J.T. Ikin.

LEN HUTTON AND DOUGLAS JARDINE. Len Hutton of Yorkshire with Douglas Jardine of Surrey at the Scarborough Festival in 1958. Len Hutton scored a record 364 for England versus Australia at the Oval in 1938 out of an England total of 903 for 7.

This card does not necessarily include the fall of the last wicket

Surrey County Cricket Club
KENNINGTON OVAL

3D.

SURREY v. AUSTRALIANS
Wednesday, May 16th, 1956 (3 Day Match)

AUSTRALIANS		First Innings		Second Innings	
1 J. W. Burke	New South Wales	lbw b Laker	28	c & b Lock	20
2 C. C. McDonald	Victoria	c Swetman, b Laker	89	c Laker, b Lock	45
3 K. Mackay	Queensland	c Surridge, b Laker	4	lbw b Laker	4
4 R. N. Harvey	Victoria	c Constable, b Laker	13	c May, b Lock	10
5 K. R. Miller	New South Wales	not out	57	c Swetman, b Lock	2
‡6 L. Maddocks	Victoria	b Laker	12	c Laker, b Lock	0
8 R. R. Lindwall	Queensland	b Laker	0	c Constable, b Lock	4
*9 I. W. Johnson	Victoria	c Swetman, b Laker	0	run out	5
7 A. K. Davidson	New South Wales	c May, b Laker	21	c May, b Laker	7
10 P. Crawford	New South Wales	b Laker	16	not out	5
11 J. Wilson	South Australia	c Swetman, b Laker	4	st Swetman, b Lock	1
		B4 , l-b8 , w , n-b3	15	B , l-b4 , w , n-b	4
		Total	259	Total	107

FALL OF THE WICKETS

1—62	2—93	3—125	4—151	5—173	6—173	7—175	8—199	9—217	10—259
1—56	2—73	3—83	4—85	5—85	6—89	7—92	8—101	9—104	10—107

BOWLING ANALYSIS	First Innings						Second Innings					
	O.	M.	R.	W.	Wd.	N.b.	O.	M.	R.	W.	Wd.	N.b.
Loader	15	4	30	0		2	2	2	0	0		
Surridge	8	2	8	0			1		0	0		
Laker	46	18	88	10			25	10	42	2		
Lock	33	12	100	0			31.1	9	49	7		
Cox	5	0	18	0		1						
Clark							8	4	12	0		

J. C. Laker's Bowling Record
1st innings
10 wickets for 88 runs

SURREY		First Innings		Second Innings	
1 Fletcher, D. G. W.		c Maddocks, b Johnson	29	not out	9
2 Clark, T. H.		c Maddocks, b Burke	58	not out	8
3 Constable, B.		c & b Johnson	109		
4 P. B. H. May		st Maddocks b Johnson	27		
5 Barrington, K.		c Miller, b Johnson	4		
‡7 Swetman, R.		st Maddocks, b Davidson	0		
11 Cox, D. F.		b Davidson	13		
6 Laker, J. C.		c McDonald, b Johnson	43		
*8 W. S. Surridge		c Harvey, b Johnson	38		
9 Lock, G. A. R.		b Davidson	0		
10 Loader, P. J.		not out	12		
		B10, l-b3 , w1 , n-b	14	B1 , l-b1 , w , n-b 1	3
		Total	347	Total (0 wkts.)	20

FALL OF THE WICKETS

1—53	2—112	3—147	4—192	5—195	6—221	7—278	8—302	9—313	10—347
1—	2—	3—	4—	5—	6—	7—	8—	9—	10—

BOWLING ANALYSIS	First Innings						Second Innings					
	O.	M.	R.	W.	Wd.	N.b.	O	M.	R.	W.	Wd.	N.b.
Lindwall	2	1	10	0			8	4	8	0		
Crawford	1	0	4	0			7	3	9	0		1
Johnson	60.3	12	168	0								
Davidson	44	14	101	3								
Wilson	19	9	34	0	1							
Burke	7	2	16	1								

*Captain ‡Wkt.-keeper

Toss won by—Australians

Umpires—McCanlis & Gray

Result—Surrey won by 10 wkts.

HOURS OF PLAY—1st & 2nd Days 11.30—6.30   3rd Day 11.0—5.0.   Lunch 1.30 All Days

Printed on the ground by the Surrey County Cricket Club Printing Department

SCORECARD SURREY VERSUS AUSTRALIANS 1956. This is the original fully printed up scorecard of the Surrey versus Australians Tour Match at the Oval on Wednesday 16 May 1956, day one of a three day match.

JIM LAKER. Born at Bradford in 1922, Jim Laker was an exceptionally accurate off-spin bowler, capable late order batsman and good gully fieldsman. He represented Surrey between 1946 and 1959, playing 309 first-class matches he took 1,395 wickets (av. 17.37) with a best of 10 for 88, taking 5 wickets in an innings 93 times and he scored 5,531 runs (av. 17.44) with 2 centuries of which his best score was 113. He played one season with Auckland in 1951/52 and later he played some 30 matches for Essex between 1962 and 1964 at the invitation of Trevor Bailey. Bowling in harness with Tony Lock the pair spun Surrey to seven Championships in the 1950s. Representing England in 46 Tests he took 193 wickets (av. 21.24), scored 676 runs (av. 14.08) and he toured abroad eight times. In 1956 at Old Trafford, Manchester he achieved the record breaking feat of match figures of 19 for 90 versus Australia with all 19 wickets being taken at the Stretford End of the ground. On retirement he wrote the controversial book Over to Me amongst others and was a BBC Television commentator until his death at Putney, London in 1986.

BERNARD CONSTABLE. Born at East Molesey, Surrey in 1921, Bernie Constable, brother of Dennis (Northamptonshire) was a right-handed middle order batsman, right-arm leg-break bowler and superb cover-point fieldsman. He represented the county in 434 first class matches from 1939 to 1964, scoring 18,224 runs (av. 30.37) with 26 centuries including a highest score of 205 not out versus Somerset at the Oval in 1952, took 49 wickets (av. 52.75) with a best of 3 for 68 and he held 173 catches. He achieved 1,000 runs in a season twelve times with a best of 1,799 runs (av. 39.97) in 1961. He toured Rhodesia with Surrey in 1959/60.

TONY LOCK. Born at Limpsfield, Surrey in 1929, Tony Lock was a fine left-arm leg-spinner, positive late order batsman and specialist close fielder. He represented Surrey between 1946 and 1963 where he bowled well in tandem with Jim Laker. During his career at The Oval he played 385 first-class matches for the club taking 1,713 wickets (av. 17.41) with a best of 10 for 54, achieving 5 wickets in an innings 123 times and ten wickets in a match 31 times. He also scored 5,391 runs (av. 15.35) and he held 532 catches. Whilst at the Oval he made his Test debut in 1952 for England at Old Trafford, Manchester versus India and he subsequently played in 49 Tests between 1952 and 1967/68, taking 174 wickets (av. 25.58). He toured abroad five occasions, including two trips to the Caribbean in 1953/54 and 1967/68. His best performance was 7 for 35 versus New Zealand at Old Trafford, Manchester in 1958. As a batsman, Lock's top score was 89 made batting at number 9 in his last Test versus West Indies at Georgetown, Guyana in 1967/68. Moving to Leicestershire after his 18 seasons in London at the Oval he represented the Grace Road club in 65 matches between 1965 and 1967, taking 272 wickets (av. 18.81) including a best of 8 for 85, he scored 1,325 runs (av. 18.15) and he held 79 catches predominately at leg-slip. Ending his career with Western Australia in 1970/71 he retired to live in Perth, Australia where he died in 1995.

ERIC BEDSER. Born at Reading in 1918, Eric Bedser was a right-handed top order batsman and right-arm off-break bowler. Elder twin brother of Alec he joined Surrey in 1939 and represented the county in 443 first-class matches until he retired in 1961. During his career at the Oval he accumulated 14,148 runs (av. 23.93) with 9 centuries including a top score of 163 versus Nottinghamshire at the Oval in 1949, he took 797 wickets (av. 24.88) with a best of 7 for 33 versus Leicestershire at the Oval in 1955 and he held 226 catches. He also took five wickets in an innings 24 times and ten wickets in a match 4 times. He achieved 1,000 runs in a season six times with his best season being 1949 when he scored 1,740 runs (av. 34.11). He played a single match in Australia in 1950/51 due to an emergency and toured Rhodesia with Surrey in 1959/60. His last first-class appearance was for M.C.C. in 1962. He was president of Surrey in 1990.

ROY SWETMAN. Born at Westminster, London in 1933, Roy Swetman was a lower order right-handed batsman wicket-keeper and occasional off-break bowler. Making his first-class debut for Combined Services in 1953. He joined Surrey in 1954 and represented the county in 129 first-class matches until 1961. He then moved north to Trent Bridge, where he played for Nottinghamshire in 56 matches from 1966 to 1967 before then departing and heading westwards for Bristol where he represented Gloucestershire in 45 matches between 1972 and 1974. For Surrey he achieved 267 dismissals (230 catches, 37 stumpings), scored 3.073 runs (av. 20.62) and made a highest score of 93. He represented England in 11 Tests from 1958/59 to 1959/60 achieving 26 dismissals and making a highest score of 65. He toured abroad on three occasions to Pakistan 1955/56, Australia and New Zealand 1958/59 and West Indies 1959/60.

THOMAS CLARK. Born at Luton, Bedfordshire in 1924, Tom Clark was a sound top order right-handed batsman and right-arm off-break bowler. He joined Surrey in 1947 after playing one season of minor county cricket for his native Bedfordshire. He represented Surrey in 260 first-class matches until 1959/60, scoring 11,458 runs (av. 29.68) with 12 centuries including a top score of 191 versus Kent at Blackheath in 1956, took 73 wickets (av. 30.58) with a best of 5 for 23 versus Middlesex at Lord's in 1952 and he held 104 catches. He achieved 1,000 runs in a season six times with a best of 1,570 runs (av. 32.70) in 1957. Forced to retire in 1957 because of arthritis, his benefit match at Wardown Park, Luton in 1961 attracted a crowd of some 6,000. He also played soccer for Walsall and Aston Villa. He died at Luton in 1981.

ARTHUR PARSONS. Born at Guildford, Surrey in 1933, Arthur Parsons was a steady top order right-handed batsman and leg-break bowler. He attended Brighton School before graduating to Cambridge University for whom he played between 1964 and 1955, achieving a Blue in both years. He joined the county in 1958 and represented Surrey in 119 first-class matches until 1963. He scored 5,307 runs (av. 28.68) with 3 hundreds including a highest score of 125 versus Glamorgan at Ebbw Vale in 1961 and versus Cambridge University at Fenner's in 1962 and he also held 48 catches. He achieved 1,000 runs in a season three times and his best season was 1961 when he accumulated 1,415 runs (av. 32.15).

BARRY KNIGHT AND KEN BARRINGTON. Barry Knight of Leicestershire and Essex and Ken Barrington of Surrey walking out to bat at Scarborough during a Festival Match in 1962.

CHARITY CRICKET AT THE OVAL. Left to right, are Micky Stewart, Andy Williams, Arthur McIntyre and Vic Lewis discussing tactics prior to the Surrey versus Vic Lewis XI match at the Oval in 1972 in aid of Micky Stewart's Benefit Year.

SURREY PLAYERS WITH MUSICIAN VIC LEWIS. Surrey and Derbyshire cricketers with jazz musician, band leader and cricket lover Vic Lewis. Left to right: Cliff Gladwin, Les Jackson, Tony Lock, Alec Bedser, Vic Lewis, Eric Bedser, Dusty Rhodes, Jim Laker and George Dawkes during the county championship match at the Oval in 1952.

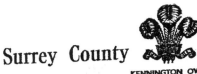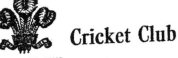

Surrey County   Cricket Club

KENNINGTON OVAL

SURREY v. LANCASHIRE
Wednesday, August 29th, 1956 (3 Day Match)

SURREY	First Innings		Second Innings
1 Clark, T. H.	c &. b Tattersall	31	
2 Stewart, M. J.	c Jordan, b Statham	5	
3 Constable, B.	b Tattersall	1	
4 P. B. H. May	c Jordan, b Hilton	1	
5 Barrington, K.	c Jordan, b Hilton	26	
6 Bedser, E. A.	lbw b Tattersall	11	
‡7 McIntyre, A. J.	lbw b Tattersall	0	
8 Laker, J. C.	c Ikin, b Tattersall	3	
*9 W. S. Surridge	c Jordan, b Hilton	10	
10 Lock, G. A. R.	c Edrich, b Tattersall	4	
11 Loader, P. J.	not out	0	B , l-b , w , n-b —
	B2 , l-b2 , w , n-b	4	
	Total	96	Total

FALL OF THE WICKETS

1—14	2—41	3—42	4—43	5—57	6—59	7—63	8—81	9—88	10—96
1—	2—	3—	4—	5—	6—	7—	8—	9—	10—

BOWLING ANALYSIS	First Innings						Second Innings					
	O.	M.	R.	W.	Wd.	N.b.	O.	M.	R.	W.	Wd.	N.b.
Statham	8	3	10	1								
Wharton	3	1	5	0								
Hilton	25.1	9	45	3								
Tattersall	21	6	32	6								

County Championship Record
SURREY CHAMPIONS [Captain: W. S. Surridge]
1952—53—54—55—56

LANCASHIRE	First Innings		Second Innings
1 Wharton, A.	c Loader, b Lock	22	
2 Dyson, J.	not out	15	
3 Edrich, G. A.	lbw b Laker	0	
*4 Washbrook, C.	not out	1	
5 Grieves, K.			
6 Ikin, J. T.			
7 Pullar, G.			
8 Hilton, M. J.			
‡9 Jordan, J.			
10 Statham, J. B.			
11 Tattersall R.			B , l-b , w , n-b —
	B2 , l-b , w , n-b	2	
	Total (2 wkts.)	40	Total

FALL OF THE WICKETS

1—37	2—37	3—	4—	5—	6—	7—	8—	9—	10—
1—	2—	3—	4—	5—	6—	7—	8—	9—	10—

BOWLING ANALYSIS	First Innings						Second Innings					
	O.	M.	R.	W.	Wd.	N.b.	O.	M.	R.	W.	Wd.	N.b.
Lock	11	5	19	1								
Laker	11	4	19	1								
Bedser (E.A.)	1	1	0	—								

*Captain   ‡Wkt.-keeper

Umpires—Langridge & McCanlis

Toss won by—LANCASHIRE

RESULT—Match Abandoned

Hours of Play—1st Day 11.30—6.30. 2nd Day 11.0—6.30. 3rd Day 11.0—5.0 or 5.30. Lunch 1.30 all days.

Printed on the ground by the Surrey County Cricket Club Printing Department

SCORECARD SURREY VERSUS LANCASHIRE MATCH 1956. The original fully printed up scorecard of the Surrey versus Lancashire County Championship match at the Kennington Oval on Wednesday 29 August 1956 when Surrey celebrated winning the county championship for the fifth consecutive year between 1952 and 1956 under the captaincy of Stuart Surridge.

SURREY TEAM 1963. Back row, left to right: A.J. McIntyre (coach), R.A.E. Tindall, J.H. Edrich, R. Harman, D.A.D. Sydenham, R.I. Jefferson, D. Gibson, M.D. Willett, S.J. Storey, A. Long (wkt-kpr.), G.G. Arnold, A.B.D. Parsons and J. Tait (masseur). Front row, left to right: W.A. Smith, K.F. Barrington, B. Constable, M.J. Stewart (captain), G.A.R. Lock, P.J. Loader and P.I. Pocock. Micky Stewart's first season as captain of the county saw Surrey finish eleventh in the championship with just 5 victories and lose to Worcestershire by 114 runs in the first round of the Gillette Cup One Day Knock-out competition at New Road, Worcester.

SURREY TEAM 1964. Back row, left to right: A. Sandham (scorer), A.J. McIntyre (coach), P.I. Pocock, K.B. McIntyre, M.J. Edwards, R. Harman, G.G. Arnold, S.J. Storey, A. Long, W.A. Smith, I.W. Finlay, L.K. Galer and J. Tait (masseur). Front row, left to right: R.A.E. Tindall, D. Gibson, K.F. Barrington, M.J. Stewart (captain), Commander B.O. Babb (secretary), B. Constable, J.H. Edrich, D.A.D. Sydenham and M.D. Willett. Despite his disappointing first season as skipper in 1963, Micky Stewart in his second year as captain led the county to fourth in the county championship with 11 victories. The County also reached the semi-final of the Gillette Cup with victories against Cheshire at Hoylake by 62 runs, Gloucestershire at the Oval by 46 runs and Middlesex at the Oval by a massive 146 runs before losing the semi-final to the eventual winners Sussex by 90 runs at Hove.

106

Seven
The Players

HENRY HARRISON. Born at Cheam, Surrey in 1883 Henry Harrison was a steady middle order right-handed batsman, slow right-arm bowler and good slip fieldsman. He represented the county from 1909 to 1923 playing 164 first-class matches. Accumulating 5,226 runs (av. 23.64) with a top score of 155 not out, he also took 20 wickets (av. 36.30) and he held 117 catches. His best season was 1913 when he scored 1,293 (av. 40.40). After retiring he acted as umpire in 1927 and he died at Bognor Regis in 1971.

TOM RICHARDSON. Born at Byfleet in 1870, Tom Richardson was a tall strong right-arm fast bowler who represented the county from 1892 to 1904 during which time he took 1,005 wickets in four consecutive seasons. He took a record 290 wickets in 1895 and ended his career with a massive 1,775 wickets (av. 17.87) for the county. Playing 305 first-class matches for the county his best bowling performance was 10 for 45 versus Essex at the Oval in 1894 and he achieved 10 wickets in a match 60 times and 5 wickets in an innings 169 times. Equally striking in Tests he played 14 matches for England, touring abroad twice between 1893 and 1897/98. He took 88 wickets (av. 25.22) with a best of 8 for 94 versus Australia at Sydney in 1897/98. He later represented London County in 1904 and in 1905 he became a publican in Bath. He died aged 42 while on holiday in the French Mountains at St Jean D'Arvey, Savoie in 1912.

MAURICE READ. Born at Thames Ditton in 1859, the nephew of H.H. Stephenson, Maurice Read was an aggressive right-handed batsman, occasional right-arm medium pace bowler and an accurate fielder. He represented the county between 1880 and 1895 and was an immensely popular character with fellow professionals and followers of the game. Scoring four double hundreds in 278 first-class matches he made a total of 10,840 runs (av. 26.12) with 8 hundreds, he bagged 64 wickets (av. 25.15) with a best of 6 for 41 and he held 165 catches. Representing England in 17 Tests from 1882-93 he scored 463 runs (av. 17.14) with a highest score of 57 versus Australia at Adelaide in 1891/92 and he toured abroad 5 times. When he retired from cricket in 1895 he worked on the Tichborne Estate and died at Winchester in 1929.

WALTER READ. Born at Reigate in 1855, Walter Read was a right-handed batsman, right-arm medium bowler, who later bowled slow lobs and an aggressive point fieldsman. Playing 366 first-class matches for the county he accumulated 17,683 runs (av. 32.80) with 31 centuries and a highest score of 338 in 390 minutes versus Oxford University at the Oval in 1888. He was the first player to score a double century in successive innings for Surrey in 1887. Making his Test debut in 1882/83 he toured abroad three times and appeared in 18 Tests for England, scoring 720 runs (av. 27.69) with a single century, 117 made at number 10 versus Australia at the Oval in 1884 when demoted in the batting order by Lord Harris. He twice captained England winning both Tests although he was never given the command of his county. He died at Addiscombe in 1907.

JACK CRAWFORD. Born at Cane Hill in 1886 and educated at Repton School, Jack Crawford followed his father, uncle and two brothers into county cricket. A remarkable, bespectacled right-handed all-rounder, he made his Surrey debut at 17 years, taking 10 for 78 versus Gloucestershire in 1904 and he was the youngest player until Brian Close in 1949 to complete the double. Representing Surrey between 1904 and 1921, he played 120 first-class matches accumulating 5,217 runs (av. 32.60) with 8 centuries and a top score of 232. He took 450 wickets (av. 19.47) with a best of 8 for 24. Playing for England from 1905/06 to 1907/08 he toured abroad twice and in total he scored 469 runs (av. 22.33) and he took 39 wickets (av. 29.48). He left Surrey after a dispute, to become assistant master at St Peter's College in Adelaide and during this period abroad he represented teams in both Australia and New Zealand. Namely; South Australia 1909/10 and 1913/14, Otago 1914/15, Wellington 1917/18 and a tour for Australia to New Zealand in 1913/14, before settling his differences with the county and returning to the Oval in 1919. He died at Epsom in 1963.

JOHN RAPHAEL. Born at Brussels, Belgium in 1882, John Raphael was an attacking right-handed top order batsman and slow medium right-arm bowler. He learned his early cricket at Merchant Taylors' School, before going up to Oxford University where he obtained Blues in 1903, 1904 and 1905. He represented Surrey in 39 first-class matches from 1903 to 1909, scoring 1,614 runs (av. 28.31) with a top score of 111, he also held 15 catches. Captaining Surrey during the latter part of the 1904 season he also played for London County in 1901 and 1902. His best season was 1904 when he amassed 1,695 runs (av. 39.41) with a career best score of 201 for Oxford University versus Yorkshire at the Parks. A full England rugby international he won 9 caps at three-quarter back and stood as a Liberal candidate for Croydon but was not elected. He died at Remy, Belgium in 1917 from wounds received in the Battle of Messines Ridge.

ARTHUR GILLIGAN. Born at Denmark Hill, London in 1894, Arthur Gilligan was a right-handed middle order batsman, right-arm fast medium bowler and good fieldsman. The brother of A.H.H. (Sussex) and F.W. (Essex) he represented Surrey in only three first-class matches in 1919, scoring 33 runs (av. 6.60), taking three wickets and holding a single catch. He moved to Sussex in 1920 and played 227 first-class matches for the seaside county until his retirement in 1932. He captained the county from 1922 to 1929. He played 11 Tests for England, 9 as Captain, from 1922/23 to 1924/25 and he toured abroad three times. During his career he amassed 9,140 runs (av. 20.08) and he bagged 868 wickets (av. 23.20) with a best of 8 for 25. His best Test performances were 39 not out and 6 for 7. After retiring he was a respected cricket administrator for both Sussex and M.C.C. He died at Mare Hill, Pulborough in 1976.

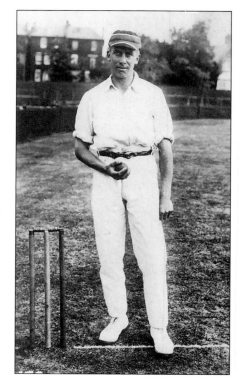

LEN BRAUND. Born at Clewer, Berkshire in 1875, Leonard Braund was a middle order right-handed batsman, leg-break bowler and excellent slip fieldsman. He represented Surrey in 21 first-class matches between 1896 and 1898, during which time he scored 409 runs (av. 15.73) with a highest score of 85, took just two wickets and held a single catch. After little success at the Oval, in 1899 he moved westwards to Somerset, for whom he played 281 first-class matches until his retirement in 1920. He also represented London County from 1900 to 1904. During his career he amassed 17,801 runs (av. 25.61) with a top score of 257 not out for Somerset versus Worcestershire at Worcester in 1913 and he took 1,114 wickets (av. 38.51) with a best of 9 for 41 for Somerset versus Yorkshire at Bramall Lane, Sheffield in 1902. He played 23 Tests for England from 1901/02 to 1907/08, touring three times he scored 987 runs (av. 25.97) with a best of 104 and he took 47 wickets (av. 38.51) with a best of 8 for 81. He died at Putney Common, London in 1955.

THOMAS SHEPHERD. Born at Headington Quarry, Oxfordshire in 1889 Thomas Shepherd was a sound middle-order right-handed batsman, right-arm medium pace bowler and superb slip fieldsman. He represented Surrey in 354 first-class matches from 1919 to 1932, scoring 18,254 runs (av. 39.68) with 41 centuries and a top score of 277 not out versus Gloucestershire at the Oval in 1927. He also took 439 wickets (av. 30.70) with a best of 6 for 78 and he held 267 catches. Hitting five double centuries for the county, he achieved 1,000 runs in a season twelve times with his best season being 1927 when he amassed 2,145 runs (av. 55.00). He died at Norbiton, Surrey in 1957.

THOMAS RUSHBY. Born at Cobham, Surrey in 1880 Thomas Rushby was a right-arm fast-medium bowler and right-handed tail end batsman. He represented the county between 1903 and 1921 playing 228 first-class matches, he took 954 wickets (av. 20.48) with a best of 10 for 43 versus Somerset at Taunton in 1921. He achieved 5 wickets in an innings 58 times, scored 1,192 runs (av. 7.45) with a highest score of 58 not out and he also held 64 catches. His best season was 1911 when he bagged 132 wickets (av. 21.71). He died at Ewell, Surrey in 1962.

ALAN PEACH. Born at Maidstone in 1890 Alan Peach was a middle or late order right-handed batsman, right-arm medium pace bowler and good fieldsman. He represented Surrey between 1919 and 1931 in 324 first-class matches scoring 8,497 runs (av. 23.53) with a top score of 200 not out versus Northamptonshire at Northampton in 1920. He also took 778 wickets (av. 26.04) with a best of 8 for 60 and he held 177 catches. In 1929/30 he toured Jamaica with Sir Julien Cahn's XI and after playing a couple of seasons with Berkshire in 1933-34 he coached the county from 1935 to 1939. He died at Newbury, Hampshire in 1961.

MILES HOWELL. Born at Thames Ditton, Surrey in 1893 the son of Reginald the former Surrey player (1878-79), Miles Howell was an opening right-handed batsman and brilliant outfielder. Learning his cricket, like many, at Repton School he went on to achieve Blues at Oxford in 1914 and 1919 when he was captain of the University team. He represented Surrey from 1919 to 1925 in 36 first-class matches, scoring 1,117 runs (av. 23.76) with a top score of 99. In 1922 he played for the Combined Universities versus Glamorgan under the captaincy of W. Osborne. A noted amateur International footballer, he won caps against Ireland, Wales, Belgium (as captain) and France between 1919 and 1920 during which time he also represented the Corinthian Casuals. He died at Worplesdon, Surrey in 1976.

ALAN MARSHAL. Born at Warwick, Queensland, Australia in 1883 Alan Marshal was a hard-hitting right-handed middle order batsman, right-arm fast-medium bowler and good close fieldsman. He represented his native Queensland 11 times in 1903/04 and 1913/14 before coming to England in 1904 to qualify by residence for Surrey. He represented the county from 1907 to 1910 in 98 first-class matches scoring 4,195 runs (av. 28.53) with a top score of 176, took 101 wickets (av. 21.00) with a best of 7 for 41 and he held 90 catches. He achieved 1,000 runs in a season three times with his best season being 1908 when he amassed 1,931 runs (av. 40.22). Suspended by the Surrey committee in 1909 he returned to Australia in 1910 and he died in Imtarfa, Malta in 1915 of enteric fever.

HERBERT STRUDWICK. Born at Mitcham in 1880, Herbert 'Struddy' Strudwick joined Surrey in 1898 and he served the county club for 60 years. Until surpassed by J.T. Murray in 1975 and subsequently by R.W. Taylor in 1982, he held the record for the most dismissals in first-class cricket 1,477 (1,242 catches, 255 stumpings) achieved in 675 matches. He also scored 5,485 runs (av. 11.01) with a top score of 93 and took a record number of dismissals for the county 1,223 (1,040 catches, 183 stumpings). A popular and respected cricketer he later acted as coach and scorer for the county while running the South London Cricket School with Andy Sandham. Had his batting been better he would have probably played more than 28 Tests for England as his place was often taken by `Tiger' Smith or A.A. Lilley of Warwickshire who were superior batsman. He died at Shoreham-by-Sea in 1970.

ANDY SANDHAM. Born at Streatham in 1890, Andy Sandham served Surrey for 60 years as a sound opening batsman and outstanding deep fieldsman between 1911 and 1937, coach from 1946 to 1958 and scorer between 1959 and 1970. A small neat batsman he was a fine player of quick bowling and he formed a formidable partnership with Jack Hobbs for 15 years. Playing 525 first-class matches for the county he scored 33,312 runs (av. 43.88) with 83 centuries and he shared 63 century opening stands with 'The Master' and he also held 129 catches. His best season was 1929 when he amassed 2,565 runs. Although he represented England in 14 Tests in 10 years, he never opened for his country due to the presence of Herbert Sutcliffe. Representing England from 1921 to 1929/30 he scored 879 runs (av. 38.21) including the first triple century in Test Cricket made in his final Test, 325 in 10 hours versus the West Indies at Kingston, Jamaica in 1929/30. He died at Westminster in 1982.

ANDREW DUCAT. Despite playing only one Test Match for England, Andy Ducat the footballer, photographed here, was capped by his country six times. He represented England against Scotland, Wales and Northern Ireland in 1910, Scotland and Wales in 1921 and Northern Ireland in 1922. On the domestic front he appeared for Aston Villa whom he led to the F.A. Cup in 1920 beating Huddersfield Town 1-0 after extra time, Southend United, Woolwich Arsenal and Fulham during his career.

ARTHUR McINTYRE. Born at Kennington, London in 1918, Arthur McIntyre was a lower middle order right-handed batsman, right-arm leg-break bowler and wicket-keeper. He represented Surrey in 376 first-class matches from 1938 to 1963 during which time he scored 10,893 runs (av. 23.22) with 7 centuries including a highest score of 143 not out, achieved 762 dismissals (617 catches, 145 stumpings) and even took 4 wickets (av. 45.00). He achieved 1,000 runs in a season three times with a best of 1,200 runs (av. 24.48) in 1949. Playing 3 Tests for England between 1950 and 1955 he toured Australia and New Zealand in 1950/51 as second choice wicket-keeper. Appointed county coach at the end of the 1958 season whilst still playing he later became cricket manager before handing over to Micky Stewart in 1978.

ALFRED GOVER. Born at Epsom, Surrey in 1908, Alf Gover was a right-arm fast bowler and lower order right-handed batsman. He represented the county in 336 first-class matches from 1928 to 1947 during which time he had taken 1,437 wickets (av. 23.73) with a best of 8 for 34, including 5 wickets in an innings 87 times and 10 wickets in a match 15 times. He achieved 100 wickets in a season eight times, achieving 200 wickets in a season twice, and his best season was 201 wickets (av. 18.98) in 1937. He also scored 2,170 runs (av. 9.35) with a top score of 41 not out and he held 164 catches. He represented England in just 4 Tests between 1936 and 1946 his best bowling performance was 3 for 85. Touring India with Lord Tennyson in 1937/38 he made his final appearance for an England XI versus Glamorgan in 1948. In his retirement he has for many years been involved with the South London Indoor Cricket School. He was president of the county in 1980 and in his early career was a noted amateur football goal-keeper for the Corinthian Casuals.

ALEC BEDSER CBE. Born in Reading in 1918, Alec Bedser was a well built right-arm fast medium bowler who was rated by Don Bradman as the most difficult bowler he ever faced. A most useful right-handed batsman he was often called upon as night-watchman for Surrey and England. In total he played 371 first-class matches for the county taking 1,459 wickets (av. 19.13), he scored 4,108 runs (av. 14.61) and he held 228 catches. He represented England in 51 Tests taking 236 wickets (av. 24.89) with match figures of 14 for 99 versus Australia at Trent Bridge, Nottingham in 1953. He also scored 714 runs (av. 12.75) and he toured abroad on eight occasions with M.C.C. After retiring from the game he acted as Chairman of the England Selectors between 1969 and 1981. Later he managed two M.C.C. tours abroad and was President of the Surrey C.C.C. in 1987.

KEN BARRINGTON. Born at Reading in 1930, Ken Barrington was a courageous stocky right-handed middle order batsman, expert slip fielder and occasional right-arm leg-break and googly bowler. He played 362 first-class matches for the county from 1953 until he suffered a mild heart attack and retired in 1968. He amassed 19,197 runs (av. 41.28) with 43 centuries, took 133 wickets (av. 35.55) with a best of 5 for 46 and he held 381 catches. He represented England in 82 Tests accumulating 6,806 runs (av. 58.67) with 20 centuries, making a top score of 256 against Australia at Old Trafford in 1964. He was the first cricketer to score a century for England in all 7 Test playing countries and he also took 29 wickets (av. 44.82). In all he toured abroad with England on 11 occasions and was assistant manager of the England tour of the West Indies in 1981/82 when he died of a heart attack at Needham's Point, Bridgetown, Barbados.

DAVID FLETCHER. Born at Sutton, Surrey in 1924, David Fletcher was a stylish opening right-handed batsman. He represented the county in 300 first-class matches from 1946 to 1961, scoring 13,646 runs (av. 30.05) with 21 centuries including a highest score of 194 and he held 174 catches. He achieved 1,000 runs in a season four times with a best of 1,960 runs (av. 37.69) in 1952. He toured abroad twice with a Commonwealth team to India in 1953/54 and with the county to Rhodesia in 1959/60 although he would have been destined for further honours in the game but for illness and injuries.

PETER MAY CBE. Born at Reading in 1929, Peter May was coached at Charterhouse School by George Geary of Leicestershire and he played for Berkshire at 16 years of age. He made his first-class debut for Combined Services, before going up to Cambridge University where he attained Blues in 1950, 1951 and 1952. He was considered the most talented right-handed stroke making batsman to play in his era. Representing the County from 1950 to 1963 he played 208 first-class scoring games 14,168 runs (av. 50.41) with 39 centuries and he held 182 catches. He represented England in 66 Tests, captaining in 41, with 21 wins and he toured abroad seven times. In his first Test at Headingley, Leeds in 1951 versus South Africa he scored 138. In total he accumulated 4,537 runs (av. 46.77). His highest score was 285 not out versus the West Indies at Edgbaston, Birmingham in 1957. Since retiring at 31 he has concentrated on committee work and was an England selector between 1965 and 1968 and again between 1982 and 1988 as chairman. President elect of the county, he died in 1994.

PETER LOADER. Born at Wallington in 1929, Peter Loader was a right-arm fast bowler who represented the county between 1951 and 1963 where he formed part of the famous quartet (Bedser, Laker, Lock and Loader). Representing Surrey in 298 first-class matches 1,108 wickets (av. 18.66) with a best of 9 for 17 versus Warwickshire at the Oval in 1958 and he accumulated 1,827 runs (av. 8.95). Making his Test debut versus Pakistan at the Oval in 1954 he represented England in 13 Tests taking 39 wickets (av. 22.51) with a best of 6 for 36 versus the West Indies at Headingley, Leeds in 1957 including the first hat trick (Goddard, Ramadhin and Gilchrist) in a home series since 1899. He toured abroad six times and later emigrated after retiring from first-class cricket to run a successful transport business in Western Australia where he represented the State during the season 1963/64.

MICHAEL WILLETT. Born at West Norwood, London in 1933, Mike Willett was a middle order right-handed batsman and a right-arm medium pace bowler. Joining the county in 1955 he played 172 first-class matches for Surrey until his retirement in 1967. He took 6,535 runs (av. 28.66) with 8 hundreds including a top score of 126 versus Kent at the Oval in 1961 and versus Hampshire at Bournemouth in 1964, took 23 wickets (av. 48.04) and held 95 catches. He achieved 1,000 runs in a season three times with a best of 1,789 runs (av. 45.87) in 1964. During the off-season he played regular amateur soccer as inside-right for the Corinthian Casuals.

RAMAN SUBBA ROW CBE. Born at Streatham in 1932 Raman Subba Row was a sound left-handed top order batsman, slow leg-break and googly bowler and fine slip fieldsman. He attended Whitgift School prior to making his debut for Cambridge University, where he obtained Blues in the three years 1951-53. He represented Surrey in 41 matches between 1953 and 1954 scoring 1,663 runs (av. 35.38) with 3 centuries and a top score of 128, before heading north to Northamptonshire where he played 133 matches between 1955 and 1961. His career's best score was 300 for Northamptonshire versus Surrey at the Oval in 1958. With his slow bowling he took just a single wicket for Surrey but his best of 5 for 21 was for Cambridge University versus Oxford University in the varsity match at Lord's in 1951. He achieved 1,000 runs in a season six times with a best of 1,917 (av. 46.75) in 1959. Captaining Northamptonshire between 1958 and 1961 he also played 13 Tests for England between 1958 and 1961, scoring 984 runs (av. 46.85) with a top score of 137 versus Australia at the Oval in 1961. He toured abroad three times, twice as a player and once as manager to India in 1981/82. He was chairman of Surrey between 1974 and 1978 and chairman of the TCCB and the Cricket Council between 1985 and 1990. He has recently acted as referee at Test Matches around the world.

MICKY STEWART. Born at Herne Hill in 1932, Micky Stewart was an outstanding sportsman at Alleyns School. A right-handed batsman and brilliant close fielder he represented the county from 1954 to 1972 being captain between 1963 and 1972. Playing 498 matches for the county he scored 25,007 runs (av. 33.20) with 48 centuries and he held 604 catches. At Northampton in 1957 he achieved a world record 7 catches in an innings and ended the season with 77 catches, taken mainly at gully. His best season was 1962 when he accumulated 2,045 runs. An England amateur football international at inside-right he also played 11 games, scoring a single goal, for Charlton Athletic between 1956-59 with fellow cricketers Stuart Leary, Derek Ufton and Sid O'Linn. He represented England in 8 Tests between 1962 and 1963/64 scoring 385 runs (av. 35.00) with a highest score of 87 versus the West Indies at Old Trafford, Manchester in 1963 and he toured abroad on nine occasions. Since his retirement he has acted as Surrey coach, England manager and he is presently based at the National Cricket Association.

RONALD TINDALL. Born at Streatham, London in 1935, Ron Tindall was a middle order right-handed batsman and right-arm off-break bowler. He represented the county in 172 first-class matches between 1956 and 1966, scoring 5,383 runs (av. 24.69) with a top score of 109 not out, took 150 wickets (av. 32.30) with a best of 5 for 41 and he held 129 catches. His best season was 1963 when he scored 1,126 runs (av. 28.15). A good soccer player he represented Chelsea, West Ham United, Reading and Portsmouth as a centre forward.

DAVID SYDENHAM. Born at Surbiton, Surrey in 1934, David Sydenham was a lower order right-handed batsman and left-arm fast-medium bowler. He represented Surrey between 1957 and 1972 in 142 first-class matches, taking 481 wickets (av. 19.85) with a best of 9 for 70 versus Gloucestershire at the Oval in 1964, scored 483 runs (av. 7.20) and he held 52 catches. He achieved 100 wickets in a season, twice with his best season being 1962 when he took 115 wickets (av. 17.65). After the 1965 season he only made one more appearance for the county in 1972.

DAVID GIBSON. Born at Mitcham, Surrey in 1936, David Gibson was a right-arm fast-medium bowler and a lower order right-handed batsman. He played for Surrey from 1957 to 1969 in 183 first-class matches, taking 550 wickets (av. 22.20) with a best of 7 for 26 versus Derbyshire at the Oval in 1960, scored 3,143 runs (av. 18.93) with a highest score of 98 versus Leicestershire at the Oval in 1965 and he held 76 catches. He took a hat-trick versus Northamptonshire and Northampton in 1961 and he later played minor county cricket for Berkshire between 1976 and 1978 before returning to the Oval as county coach from 1979 to 1983. He was also a useful full back at rugby union.

WILLIAM SMITH. Born in Salisbury, Wiltshire in 1937 William Smith was a left-handed middle order batsman and right-arm medium pace bowler. He represented Surrey between 1961 and 1970 in 144 first-class matches, scoring 5,024 runs (av. 22.42) with 2 centuries and a top score of 103 and he also took 52 catches. His best season was 1968 when he achieved 1,002 runs (av. 24.43) and after retiring he played minor county cricket for his native Wiltshire between 1971 and 1976.

MICHAEL EDWARDS. Born at Balham, London in 1940, Mike Edwards was an opening right-handed batsman, off-break bowler and good close fieldsman. He schooled at Alleyns before graduating to Cambridge University where he played between 1960 and 1962. He represented Surrey in 236 first-class matches from 1961 to 1974, scoring 10,581 runs (av. 27.06) with 12 centuries and a top score of 137 versus M.C.C. at the Oval in 1969. He also held 262 catches. He achieved 1,000 runs in a season five times with his best season being 1969 when he accumulated 1,428 runs (av. 36.61). He toured abroad twice to Pakistan in 1967/68 and West Indies in 1969/70 with Commonwealth and the Duke of Norfolk's teams. Since retiring he has served the county club as County Cricket Development Officer.

JOHN EDRICH. Born at Blofield, Norfolk in 1937 John Edrich represented Surrey between 1958 and 1978 as a left-handed opening batsman and specialist gully fieldsman. He achieved 2,000 runs in a season on six occasions and he played 410 first-class matches for the county, scoring 29,305 runs (av. 46.07) with 81 centuries and a top score of 226 not out and he also held 243 catches. Captaining the county between 1973 and 1977 and on one occasion England, he also acted as an England Selector in 1981 as a result of the untimely death of Ken Barrington. His best Test innings was in 1965 when he hit 310 not out versus New Zealand at Headingley, Leeds with a record 57 boundaries. Making 77 Test appearances he scored 5,138 runs (av. 43.54) with 12 centuries, held 43 catches and he toured abroad thirteen times. He achieved one hundred first-class centuries in 1978 against Derbyshire at the Oval and he was the first batsman to record a fifty and take the 'Man of the Match' award in a one day international, versus Australia at Melbourne in 1970/71. He is presently a batting coach for the England team.

JOHN EDRICH CENTURY OF CENTURIES PLATE. This plate celebrating John Edrich's Hundred First-Class Hundreds was produced in 1978 by Nubern Products in recognition of the feat.

ARNOLD LONG. Born at Cheam, Surrey in 1940, Arnold Long was a lower order left-handed batsman and wicket-keeper. He represented the county in 352 first-class matches between 1960 and 1975, scoring 4,999 runs (av. 15.67) with a top score of 92, he also achieved 805 dismissals (702 catches, 103 stumpings). He moved to Hove in 1976 where he represented Sussex in 97 matches, acting as captain for two seasons until his retirement in 1980. In his last season for the seaside county he led Sussex to the Gillette Cup against Somerset at Lord's. In 1964 he created a first-class record by taking 11 catches for Surrey versus Sussex at Hove. A good soccer player he represented the Corinthian Casuals. He is presently a committee member of the county club.

PAT POCOCK. Born at Bangor, North Wales in 1946, Pat 'Percy' Pocock was an aggressive off-break bowler and a late order right-handed batsman. Representing Surrey from 1964 to 1986 he played 485 first-class matches for the county taking 1,399 wickets (av. 25.43) with a best of 9 for 57 versus Glamorgan at Sophia Gardens, Cardiff in 1979 and he scored 4,400 runs (av. 12.25). His best season was 1967 when he achieved 112 wickets and his most dramatic spell of bowling was at the Saffrons, Eastbourne in 1972 when he took 7 Sussex wickets in the space of just 11 balls. Representing England in 25 Tests between 1967/68 and 1984/85 he took 67 wickets (av. 44.41) with a best performance of 6 for 79 versus Australia at Old Trafford, Manchester in 1968 and he toured abroad twelve times. He was recalled to the England team in 1984 after an interval of 86 Tests. A most popular and conscientious cricketer he led the county in his last season 1986.

GRAHAM ROOPE. Representing Surrey between 1964 and 1982, Graham Roope was born at Fareham in 1946 and was a stylish right-handed middle order batsman, excellent close fieldsman and right-arm medium pace bowler. Educated at Bradfield College he represented Berkshire before and after his career with Surrey. Playing 342 first-class matches for the county he scored 16,226 runs (av. 37.21) with 22 centuries and a highest score of 171. He also took 211 wickets (av. 36.61) with a best of 5 for 14 and he held 513 catches. A useful footballer he kept goal for Corinthian Casuals and was also an emergency wicket-keeper particularly in one day matches. As an all-rounder he would have been a more regular Test performer but for the arrival on the scene of one, Ian Botham. He played 21 Tests for England from 1972/73 to 1978 and toured abroad on nine occasions. He scored 860 runs (av. 30.710 with a highest score of 77 versus Australia at the Oval in 1975.

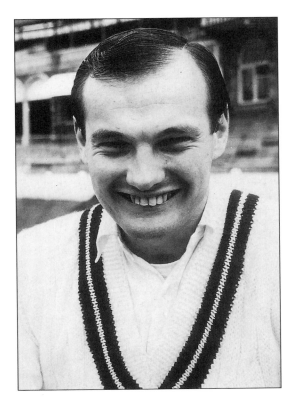

DEREK TAYLOR. Born at Amersham, Buckinghamshire in 1942, the twin brother of Michael (Nottinghamshire and Hampshire), Derek Taylor was middle or lower order, occasional opening, right-handed batsman and wicket-keeper. He represented Surrey from 1966 to 1969 in 10 first-class matches scoring 137 runs (av. 19.57) with a top score of 56 and also achieved 21 dismissals (16 catches, 5 stumpings) before moving west to Somerset whom he joined in 1970. He played for Somerset until 1982 and during his career he achieved 705 dismissals (621 catches, 84 stumpings). His best season with the bat was 1975 when he scored 1,121 runs (av. 28.02). He also represented his native Buckinghamshire between 1961 and 1963, Griqualand West in South Africa between 1970/71 and 1971/72 and also played some soccer for Corinthian Casuals while in London.

STUART STOREY. Born at Worthing in 1941, Stuart Storey was a middle order right-handed batsman, right-arm medium pace bowler and good fieldsman. He represented Surrey in 315 first-class matches between 1960 and 1974 before moving to his native Sussex in 1978 for whom he played just 16 matches. For Surrey he scored 10,402 runs (av. 25.37) with 12 centuries and a highest score of 164, he took 490 wickets (av. 216.33) with a best of 8 for 22 and he held 318 catches. He achieved 1,000 runs in a season five times with his best summer being 1971 when he amassed 1,184 runs (av. 35./87). He achieved the double in 1966 when he also took 104 wickets (av. 18.39). He later coached Sussex between 1979 and 1986.

GEOFF ARNOLD. Born at Earlsfield in 1944, Geoff Arnold was a dangerous right-arm fast-medium new ball bowler and a right-handed late order batsman. Nicknamed 'Horse' after his initials (GG), he represented Surrey between 1963 and 1977 and he then moved to Sussex for whom he played from 1978 until his retirement in 1982. Playing 218 first-class matches for Surrey he took 745 wickets (av. 19.94) with a best haul of 8 for 41. He also scored 2,302 runs (av. 13.95) and he held 78 catches. Making his Test debut versus Pakistan at Trent Bridge, Nottingham in 1967 he toured abroad eight times and he represented England in 34 Tests, taking 115 wickets (av. 28.29) with best figures of 6 for 45 versus India at Delhi in 1972/73. He remains the only bowler to have twice taken a wicket with the very first ball of a Test Match, his victims being Gavaskar and Morrison. On retiring he became coach of Surrey and is now carrying out a similar duty with Durham after having served England and Gloucestershire as bowling advisor as well.

INTIKHAB ALAM. Born at Hoshiarpur, India in 1941, Intikhab Alam was a middle order right-handed batsman and leg break and googly bowler. He represented Surrey in 232 first-class matches between 1969 and 1981 scoring 5,707 runs (av. 19.47) with 4 centuries and including a top score of 139, took 629 wickets (av. 30.00) including a best of 8 for 74 and he also held 73 catches. His best season was 1971 when he bagged 104 wickets (av. 28.36). He led Pakistan in 17 of his 47 Tests and acted as manager of Pakistan's tours to England in 1982 and 1992.

YOUNIS AHMED. Born at Jullundur, India in 1947, Younis Ahmed, brother of Saeed (Pakistan), a left-handed top order batsman and left-arm medium or slow bowler, he represented the county from 1965 to 1978 in 262 first-class matches. During his time at the Oval he accumulated 14,112 runs (av. 36.65) with 19 centuries and a top score of 183 not out. He also took 17 wickets (av. 35.41) and he held 141 catches. He also represented Lahore from 1963/64 to 1986/87, Karachi 1967/68 and P.I.A. 1969/70 in Pakistan domestic cricket. He played 4 Tests for Pakistan from 1969/70 to 1986/87 scoring only 177 runs (av. 29.50). He played 6 matches for South Australia in 1972/73, 85 matches for Worcestershire between 1979 and 1983 and 58 matches for Glamorgan from 1984 to 1986. He toured abroad seven times with various teams and his career best score was 221 not out for Worcestershire versus Nottinghamshire at Trent Bridge, Nottingham in 1979. He now lives in South Africa.

ROGER KNIGHT. Born at Streatham, London in 1946, Roger Knight was a middle order left-handed batsman and right-arm medium pace bowler. Learning his early cricket at Dulwich College, he later played for Cambridge University from 1967 to 1970, achieving Blues in all four years. He joined Surrey in 1968 and he represented the county in 174 first-class matches, captaining the county from 1978 to 1983, until his retirement in 1984. He left the county after three seasons, in 1971 to join Gloucestershire for whom he played 105 matches until 1975 after which he played for Sussex in 43 matches from 1976 to 1977 before returning to the Oval as skipper. Whilst with Surrey he scored 8,712 runs (av. 33.76) with 15 centuries and a top score of 142, he bagged 163 wickets (av. 34.04) with a best of 5 for 44 and he also held 137 catches. He achieved 1,000 runs in a season 13 times with a best of 1,350 runs (av. 38.57) in 1974. His last first-class match was for M.C.C. in 1989 and after a period as headmaster at Worksop College he was appointed secretary of M.C.C. at Lord's in 1994.

SURREY C.C.C. 1845-1995 150TH ANNIVERSARY PLATE.